BEYOND BANANAS AND CONDOMS

of related interest

Trans Sex
A Guide for Adults
Kelvin Sparks
ISBN 978 1 83997 043 6
eISBN 978 1 83997 044 3

Queer Sex
A Trans and Non-Binary Guide to
Intimacy, Pleasure and Relationships
Juno Roche
ISBN 978 1 78592 406 4
eISBN 978 1 78450 770 1

How to Understand Your Sexuality
A Practical Guide for Exploring Who You Are
Meg-John Barker and Alex Iantaffi
Illustrated by Jules Scheele
Foreword by Erika Moen
ISBN 978 1 78775 618 2
eISBN 978 1 78775 619 9

How to Understand Your Gender
A Practical Guide for Exploring Who You Are
Alex Iantaffi and Meg-John Barker
Illustrated by Jules Scheele
Foreword by S. Bear Bergman
ISBN 978 1 78592 746 1
eISBN 978 1 78450 517 2

BEYOND BANANAS AND CONDOMS

The LGBTQIA+ Inclusive Sex Education
You Never Got at School

DEE WHITNELL

Illustrated by Dee Whitnell

Jessica Kingsley Publishers
London and Philadelphia

First published in Great Britain in 2025 by Jessica Kingsley Publishers
An imprint of John Murray Press

1

The information contained in this book is not intended to replace the services of trained medical professionals or to be a substitute for medical advice. You are advised to consult a doctor on any matters relating to your health, and in particular on any matters that may require diagnosis or medical attention.

Content Warning: Chapter 5 contains mention of suicide, Chapter 6 contains mention of abuse and sexual assault, Chapter 8 contains mention of abortion, and Chapter 10 contains mention of sexual assault and abuse.

A CIP catalogue record for this title is available from the British Library and the Library of Congress

ISBN 978 1 80501 199 6
eISBN 978 1 80501 220 7

Printed and bound in Great Britain by Clays Ltd

Jessica Kingsley Publishers' policy is to use papers that are natural, renewable and recyclable products and made from wood grown in sustainable forests. The logging and manufacturing processes are expected to conform to the environmental regulations of the country of origin.

Jessica Kingsley Publishers
Carmelite House
50 Victoria Embankment
London EC4Y 0DZ

www.jkp.com

John Murray Press
Part of Hodder & Stoughton Ltd
An Hachette Company

The authorised representative in the EEA is Hachette Ireland,
8 Castlecourt Centre, Dublin 15, D15 XTP3, Ireland (email: info@hbgi.ie)

Contents

I have so many people I want to dedicate this book to, but I want to use this space to remember the trans youth and adults we have lost due to harassment, discrimination, laws and legislation that restricts them from living their true lives, waiting lists and a lack of sex education.

Inclusive sex education is lifesaving.

All individuals deserve access to comprehensive and inclusive sex education that reflects their experiences. Trans kids deserve access to sex education, and education as a whole.

Trans kids deserve to grow up.

Introduction

Raise your hand if you've been a victim of little to no sex education?

If your hand isn't raised, you're one of the lucky ones.

Many of us either received very poor sex ed, or no sex ed. It's difficult to find someone whose sex education was adequate, let alone comprehensive and inclusive, and it feels like a common experience to simply shrug our shoulders at how little we know about sex, our bodies, gender, identity, contraception and more. This shouldn't be the norm. We should all have access to sex education that teaches us how our bodies work, how best to keep our bodies healthy and safer, how to navigate sex and relationships and who we can talk or go to when things go in a direction we didn't expect them to go. Good sex education promotes inclusivity and diversity, it covers a variety of topics, it is presented in a way that is accessible for all individuals and is done so in a safe environment where there is no judgement. Though many of us can agree, this simply isn't the state of sex education universally, globally, at this time.

Sex education is a human right that all individuals deserve but, sadly, not all individuals receive or have a way to access it.

Why is inclusivity needed in sex ed?

Every individual, regardless of how they identify, deserves access to comprehensive, inclusive, and basically just good sex ed. As a queer and trans individual whose sex education was the classic 'condom on banana', 'don't have sex or you'll get pregnant' spiel, I had to teach myself everything I now know about queer sex ed – at the age of 21 when I finally realized I was queer. As a young queer, I got myself into dangerous sexual situations, felt unable to talk to anyone about my experiences, felt confused by my sexual feelings and had to rely on word of mouth, and later Google, porn and social media (which aren't always the safest of places to get your information from), to supplement my knowledge. I don't want anyone to feel alone on their sex ed journey, which is why I decided to write a book for all folks, but with an emphasis on LGBTQIA+ individuals because in-class sex ed is still far from the inclusive haven many of us dream for it to be. I've tried to include as much as I could, and by the time this book is in your hands, there will be things I wish I could have added or things that have changed or been updated, as well as topics I couldn't cover in as much depth as I wished I had.

Regardless of how you identify, you will meet many people throughout your life who identify in different ways to you and it's crucial we know how to navigate those relationships and situations and how best to support other people. Whether it's a family member, friend, colleague or partner, understanding different people's experiences only enhances your ability to support them.

Inclusive sex ed prepares us for the world, for life, and makes us better allies. Sex education is lifesaving as it provides us with the tools on how to navigate difficult situations and sexual encounters in a safer way. Not only that but being educated on experiences outside of our own also makes us more comfortable and confident in who we are and the world around us. We learn how to respect and accept all kinds of individuals, from all unique places, and in turn learn how we want to be respected and accepted. Sex education makes us better members of the community and society.

Who am I?

Before we go further, I should introduce myself properly.

I'm Dee; my pronouns are they/them. I'm a nonbinary, transgender, queer, neurodivergent sex educator who has been educating folks on LGBTQIA+ sex education via @s3xtheorywithdee on Instagram and TikTok for several years now. That's a lot of labels to describe myself, but funnily that's not even the half of it! I'm also the founder of the solidarity campaign *Trans Kids Deserve to Grow Up*, which seeks to provide support to our trans youth in schools inside and outside of sex education, a LGBTQIA+ journalist and now, I guess, an author.

Language use

I wanted to dedicate some time to talk about the inclusive language I use throughout this book. Inclusive language is not exclusive, and I wanted to ensure that everybody could access this book and see themselves reflected in the language. I am a big believer in blending gendered language and terms with gender-inclusive or neutral terms, because some folks do feel a great sense of connection to their gender, and that's great – even I, as a nonbinary person, feel tied to gender in some way. I'd never want to erase someone or their experience from a conversation, which is why I use phrases that combine both gendered and neutral language.

Throughout you will notice I use phrases like 'girls, women and AFAB individuals', 'boys, men and AMAB individuals', 'women and those with a vulva' and 'men and those with a penis', and although that represents most individuals, there is always room for conversation around the use of language. I use the terms AFAB (assigned female at birth) and AMAB (assigned male at birth) when talking about biological sex and assigned sex, but I also appreciate that not every individual will feel comfortable being referred to by these terms. You are completely valid in this feeling. I also use terms such as 'non-men' when discussing topics around sexual abuse or attraction. I use the term 'cisgender' and 'cis' and we will go into depth about why this term is a-ok to use. By the time this book is in your hands, some of these phrases may already be outdated, and that's ok. That's the beauty of language, we create new terms to encompass the complexities of being human every single day. So, if anything does change, I'll be sure to release a follow-up!

Throughout this book, you will see that I write non-binary as 'nonbinary'. This is just how I personally like it phrased. Some folks may prefer to write it with the hyphen, others like me choose not to! Does the hyphen matter? Well, not in this case, but, as we will learn, some terms require a space or a hyphen. What matters is that we listen to individuals and their own lived experiences, using language that they use when referring to them and their identity.

Why 'Beyond Bananas and Condoms'?

Nearly every individual I have spoken to about the sex ed they received at school (if they did receive any, that is) said they received a lesson on contraception where a condom was placed on a banana. *I can't stand this.* Not only is it such an inaccurate way of showcasing how to use an external condom, shaming those whose penis size is not that of an average banana, but it also removes the importance of seeing sex and anatomy for what it is and using accurate language around these topics. There shouldn't be metaphors in sex ed. Sex education needs to be concise and accurate, open and honest.

As a qualified sex educator, campaigner, journalist and English Grad, language is very important to me. When it comes to sex education, our use of language is crucial, lifesaving in some situations. Language has become even more crucial to navigating various spaces, including sex, since I came out as trans and nonbinary. That is why throughout this book I say things exactly as they are, use terms that are official, whilst also exploring common slang and phrases used by different communities. I use language that represents and reflects all identities when I can. Historically, sex education has left out many individuals, particularly in its use of language – LGBTQIA+ individuals, individuals of colour, individuals from different backgrounds and cultures. In this book, I want to provide information that is accessible to all, and I try to do that through the language I use. I am aware that I am a white individual, from a specific background, someone who has not medically transitioned, so of course I cannot speak for all communities or experiences.

I invite you to giggle at words, feel the blush on your face, the butterflies in your belly, but also to not avoid saying or using these words. I invite you to adopt the inclusive language I use throughout this book. The more comfortable we are using very specific language, the better protected we are, the more we can speak out when our boundaries are crossed, able to tell doctors exactly what is causing us pain and navigate our feelings about gender and sexuality and support all types of people. Language is powerful. Understanding how we use that language is also just as powerful. Practise in the mirror at home when you're alone. Get comfortable saying terms around the dinner table with your family (I have said vulva at the family dinner more times than I care to count).

This book will not assume what you already know. Anyone, at any stage of their sex education journey, will be able to take something from this book, whether it's affirming some things you are already familiar with and know lots about, or teaching you things that are completely new to you, or showing you a new angle to a topic you think you may know, perhaps through a queer lens you never considered before!

This book will go beyond what you have learnt in the classroom. It will ditch those bananas. We will go beyond the binary view of sex, gender and expression. We will go beyond yes and no within consent, exploring the complexities within Queer consent. We will go beyond heterosexual relationships between two people. We will go beyond nudes and emojis, talking about how to stay safer online, particularly as an LGBTQIA+ individual.

One step beyond!

Chapter 1
Beyond Man and Woman

What makes us **unique**? What makes **you** different from **me**?

There isn't only one thing that makes us unique. There are multiple parts of our identities that make us who we are, including, but not limited to: religion, race, where you're from, your interests, dislikes, your age, sexuality and gender identity. These are just some of the many parts of us which make us different from, or like, one another. Even identical twins have elements of their personalities that make them different from one another and that's the beauty of being human: each one of us is unique but also like one another in some degree. Several parts of our identities are also fluid, some are not set in stone and can change as we grow and experience new things. For example, someone may have a religious experience and change faith, or realize they aren't straight after having a gay awakening, or they might decide to become a vegan – like me!*

---

* A 'gay awakening' is a phrase used within the LGBTQIA+ community to discuss the moment someone realized they aren't straight. This may not necessarily mean that they realized in that moment, but it could be a memory

Your identity is as unique as fingerprints, and it can be as complex as fingerprints too. We are going to focus on four main components of our identity: gender, sex, sexuality and expression – as shown cutely on the Genderbread Person below. These components can interact with one another in a countless number of ways. Each of these layers may look different from one another, or they may all look similar. But, no matter how you mix these different layers, all the unique combinations are fabulous and valid. Your life experiences may change parts of you, and thus you will evolve slightly as you explore new parts of your identity. This first chapter will focus on gender, *going beyond man and woman.*

Gender

Gender is a person's internal and personal experiences of who they are. At birth, a child's gender is assumed based on their assigned (meaning 'given') sex at birth which a doctor or nurse

they reflect on later in life once they are 'out'. A 'gay awakening' can look very different from person to person. It could be a crush on a best friend at school or seeing a music video of a singer making out with someone of the same sex. Or, like me, it could be falling head-over-heels at the age of 12 for Ramona Flowers in *Scott Pilgrim vs The World*. Do I still have a huge crush on Ramona Flowers? Yes. But I also have crushes on *all* the characters in that movie and that's something that has slowly changed over the years, as has my sexuality. What I'm trying to say is that these layers that make us who we are are fluid, they change from year to year, month to month and even day to day!

provides based on the infant's external genitalia, chromosomes and hormones. Typically, this is either 'male' or 'female'. This is known as the gender binary. 'Binary' describes anything which is made up of two parts. However, not everyone's assigned gender at birth is how they truly feel inside and not everyone fits into the gender binary of 'male' or 'female'.

In the illustration above, gender is in the brain and that's because gender is something only you can decide for yourself and only you can understand and feel. This is why some people have a different gender identity from the one assigned to them at birth. A fun phrase used by some is *'gender is between my ears, sex is between my legs'* and this is a really good starting point for understanding the difference between gender and sex (although sex, as we will explore later, is way more complicated than this).

Gender is a spectrum and there are a variety of genders out there, not only the two that you may have previously understood there to be. Within the gender spectrum, new genders are being explored and added every day which better reflect individuals' unique experiences. Micro-labels are more commonly added to the gender spectrum than umbrella terms. Hang on, let's backtrack... What's an umbrella got to do with gender?

When talking about gender identity, or sexual orientation, an umbrella term is used as a unifying term under which a group of related identities and labels belong to, and the individual identities that belong to that group are called micro-labels. Umbrella terms are labels that you most likely have heard of before and can either define or know roughly what they mean: lesbian, bisexual, gay, transgender are all umbrella terms. Micro-labels are identities that you may not be as confident defining or have even heard of before, they are more defined than umbrella terms, giving precise descriptions of an identity that highlight how that identity varies from another similar identity. Let's give some examples of umbrella terms and their little family of micro-labels.

- ◉ Gender-diverse+
  - Nonbinary
  - Trans
  - Genderfluid
  - Genderqueer
  - Gender nonconforming
  - Agender

However, as with us, these identities aren't permanently stuck as one thing or another – some micro-labels are also umbrella terms and vice versa! For example, queer is an umbrella term which has various micro-labels underneath it and bisexual can be found under the multisexual umbrella.

The layers of our identities are fluid and gender identity is no exception! Some people align with one gender their entire life, whilst others try different genders out until they find the one that fits them just right, and some people continuously change their gender identity – all of these are valid.

Labels are a great way of defining our experiences, figuring out who you are, and finding a community. For some people, labels are life-changing, giving a name to a feeling that you previously couldn't describe or put into words. But for others, labels can feel restrictive. As if being placed into a new box or category after trying so hard to get out of the previous one we were assigned at birth. Some folks choose to go label-less, not using a term to describe their gender identity or sexuality, and simply 'exist'. Some choose to only use umbrella terms. I have a love-hate relationship with labels. For a time, having very specific labels to define my experiences grounded me and allowed me to understand my feelings in a greater context, but recently, that hasn't been the case. Now, I prefer to use broader labels to describe my experience, and it allows me to feel less restricted within my identity and give me more flexibility to explore my identity beyond the limits of a label.

Cisgender

Cisgender, or cis, is a term used to describe someone who identifies with the gender they were assigned with at birth.

For example, a baby is born with a vulva and vagina and is assigned 'female' at birth, and as the child grows up, she knows in herself that she is a girl and feels like a girl, so she could be described as cisgender. The same can be said about a baby born with a penis and is assigned 'male' at birth, who grows up to identify as a boy.

Some folks, particularly trans and gender-diverse people, choose to describe their identity using these acronyms:

- ⊙ AMAB – assigned male at birth
- ⊙ AFAB – assigned female at birth
- ⊙ AGAB – assigned gender at birth.

WHY DO WE NEED CIS?

Cis and cisgender are somewhat new to our vocabulary, though they have been in use since the 1990s. We are now using the prefix cis more than ever before and some anti-trans* people aren't happy with this. The term cis is used as a neutral way of describing someone who is not 'transgender'. Previously, terms such as non-transgender or gender-normative were used, but these were problematic as they claimed that those whose gender aligned with their sex were 'normal' and those who didn't were not 'normal'.

Using the term cis shows that you are a trans ally. At the time of writing this book, anti-trans bills are on the rise, with 510 passed in the US in 2023 alone, many of which focus on language around trans identities. **We need to be clear that cis is *not* a slur.**

If someone has an issue with being referred to as cis or cisgender, there's only a few reasons for this. The first reason: they probably don't know what cis means. In this case, you can use the above definition to inform them and hopefully change their mind. Reason number two: they think they do not need a label as they are 'normal'. This plays into what we just discussed about transgender folks being perceived as 'not normal', that transgender folks need a label as they differ from the status quo. If someone says this, it *may* be purely out of lack of knowledge, and most often than not, they may not actually mean harm. Yet, there are some people who do mean harm. These people are anti-trans. And the final reason: they have been a victim of the Trans Panic

---

* I use the term 'anti-trans' when referring to those who dislike, discriminate or cause harm towards trans people because the term 'transphobia' implies fear but those who discriminate against trans folks do not 'fear' us, though they use this fear as a tactic to convince others that we are some sort of threat. We are not scary. We are not something to be feared.

we are sadly seeing waves of throughout the world at the time of writing this book. These people see anything 'trans' as an issue, something to be fixed, so they obviously wouldn't want to be given a label that relates them in any way to trans people...well, tough.

Transgender

Transgender, or trans, is a term used to describe someone whose sense of identity does not match the one they were assigned at birth.

For example, a baby is born with a penis and is assigned 'male' at birth, but as the child grows up, they do not feel comfortable being called a boy and they do not feel like a boy, but rather they feel like a girl and feel more comfortable being seen as a girl by others. The child might decide to go by a 'girl' name, and to dress in clothes that feel more feminine to them and start using she/her pronouns. This child could be described as transgender and may choose to use the label trans to define themselves.

Transgender is an umbrella term and has various micro-labels within its family:

- Trans man – A man who was assigned female at birth.
- Trans masc – A label used to describe anyone assigned female at birth who identifies with masculinity to some degree.

You might ask, 'What's the difference between a trans man and someone who is trans masc? They seem so similar...', and you would be correct, they are similar, but not the same! Someone who is trans masc may not necessarily identify as a trans man, and vice versa. A trans masc individual may enjoy masculinity, whether that's via their expression, their pronouns, their name and the language they use to describe themselves, but they may not identify as a man. Here's where micro-labels show their power; though the two labels seem similar, they are unique and allow folks to describe their gender more precisely.

- ◉ Trans woman – A woman who was assigned male at birth.
- ◉ Trans femme – A label to describe anyone assigned male at birth who identifies with femininity to some degree.

Remember: Genitals do not equal gender identity. We cannot and should not assume someone's gender identity based on what genitals they have.

THE GAP BETWEEN TRANS _ WOMAN AND TRANS _ MAN IS IMPORTANT!

This is something I only learnt about in 2021 when someone corrected a post I made on trans identities when I placed 'trans' directly next to 'woman' without the space (like this: 'transwoman'). But why was this wrong? It was wrong because 'trans' is an adjective, whilst 'woman' is a noun, so you wouldn't place them together without a space, much like you wouldn't write 'blondewoman' or 'Blackwoman'. The space is important because it affirms that trans women are women.

The 'trans' label encompasses a variety of gender-diverse labels which will all look very different, with different layer combinations. The above identities can be grouped together under the 'binary transgender' section of the trans umbrella, i.e. someone who wants to identify as the opposite binary gender to the one they were assigned at birth, so being assigned a boy at birth but wanting to identify as a girl later in life. However, not all trans people identify with binary genders and want to identify outside of them, such as this next gender identity.

Nonbinary

Nonbinary, or enby* for short, is a term used to describe someone who does not identify as either a 'boy' or a 'girl' or can be used to describe someone who fluctuates between 'boy' and 'girl'.**

I already said that nonbinary comes under the transgender umbrella, and it does, but not every nonbinary person *will* identify with the trans label. Something to note here is that you may hear this line a lot from me – that labels are personal to each individual and may mean different things to different folks. One nonbinary person may love the label trans, whilst another may not feel ready or comfortable in aligning with that label for various reasons. 'But that's confusing', you might be thinking. Yes, it is to some degree, but everyone should be allowed to identify with whichever label feels right to them, and if trans doesn't then they don't need to use it. I love the label trans, but that came after two years of becoming comfortable in myself and in my community. It wasn't an instant affirmation like the label 'nonbinary' was for me.

Sidenote: Whilst writing this book over the Christmas period, my

---

* Note: Not every nonbinary person will feel comfortable or wish to be called 'enby', it's completely down to personal preference. You can either ask the person what they prefer to be called or simply use whatever terms the individual uses to address themselves. I enjoy the term enby but that doesn't mean every nonbinary person will.

** The initial NB does not stand for nonbinary, but actually stands for 'non-Black'.

mum, for the first time ever, called me 'nonbinary' and it was the best Christmas gift I could have ever received. Whilst listening to a radio segment I had been featured on, the presenter called me 'trans', which confused my mum. 'Why are they calling you trans, you're nonbinary?' After the shock of her using my label hit me, I explained how I used both terms and why folks like me sometimes do. She continued on with her day as if nothing had happened, whilst I sat with a smile on my face, knowing how hard she was trying.

Myth: 'Nonbinary is a trend' or 'Nonbinary is new'. Nonbinary identities can be traced all the way back to 2000 BCE. Though these identities weren't called 'Nonbinary' back then because that term was only coined in the early 2000s, they certainly fall under the identities category that we know today.

Gender identity is a spectrum. Now imagine that on either end is 'boy' and 'girl' or 'man' and 'woman'. So, those who identify as nonbinary may sit on any part of the spectrum, they do not necessarily have to sit precisely centre between the two binaries. Additionally, some people may travel up and down the spectrum throughout their life, or even daily! I personally swing between the two, feeling more feminine on some days and more masculine on others, yet I'm still nonbinary. There are many nonbinary identities that describe a variety of different experiences felt by those who do not identify as the gender they were assigned with at birth.

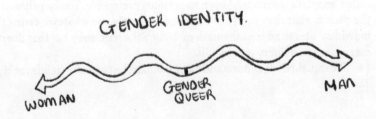

GENDER IDENTITY.

WOMAN   GENDER QUEER   MAN

NONBINARY MICRO-LABELS

We've spoken about umbrella terms and micro-labels, so let's talk about the many micro-identities that find home under the nonbinary umbrella. Here are just a few:

- ⊙ **Agender** – A term used to describe someone who has no gender, or a lack of gender.
- ⊙ **Bigender** – A term used to describe someone who experiences two genders. For example, someone who alternates between feeling like a boy and a girl could use the label bigender. This gender identity may sit in different places on the gender identity spectrum depending on how the person feels on any given day.
- ⊙ **Demigender** – A term used to describe someone who feels some, but not a full, connection to a particular gender identity. For example, someone who feels slightly like a boy, but mostly feels no gender at all, or neither like a boy or a girl, could label themselves as demigender, or more specifically **demiboy**. Someone who feels slightly like a girl, but mostly neither like a boy or a girl, could label themselves as **demigirl**.
- ⊙ **Genderfluid** – A term used to describe someone whose gender varies over time. For example, someone who sometimes feels like a girl, sometimes like a boy and sometimes like neither could label themselves as genderfluid.
- ⊙ **Genderflux** – A term used to describe someone whose gender identity fluctuates over time, whether that's in a short span of day or over a longer period. For example, someone who feels more like a girl in the morning, but throughout the day feels more like a boy, by the end of the day may identify as genderflux.

⊙ **Genderqueer** – A term used to describe someone who does not conform to conventional gender categories but identifies with neither, both or a combination of male and female genders.

⊙ **Polygender** – A term used to describe someone who experiences multiple gender identities either all at once, or at different times.

NONBINARY IDENTITIES ACROSS THE WORLD

Nonbinary identities are not confined to Western countries, but there are also different nonbinary identities across the world.

In Ghana you will find AMAB folks who deviate from normative masculinity who use the label **Kojo-besia**. In Indigenous North American cultures, you have **Two Spirit** folks who have mixed gender roles. These people express themselves and perform tasks attributed to men and women. The Bugis people of South Sulawesi, Indonesia, recognize five genders. Through a Western English-language lens, these five genders would be: trans man, trans woman, cis man, cis woman and gender-transcendent ('Bissu'). And in Italy you have the label **femminiello**, which describes someone who is assigned male at birth but has a feminine expression. And that's just a very small sample of nonbinary identities!

Pronouns

What are pronouns and why are we talking about them in this chapter?

Pronouns are sets of words that an individual wants others to use to reflect their gender identity, though pronouns aren't always an indicator of how someone identifies. We all use pronouns daily to refer to people and to ourselves. Sometimes we use them to refer to people we know, or others whom we don't. Recently, however, pronouns have become a much greater part of our vocabulary as new pronouns (or pronouns newer to us) have been introduced.

Pronouns are assigned to us at birth based on our sex, typically he/him and she/her, though later in life people may choose to use different pronouns. All of us also use 'personal pronouns': I, we, you, us, them, me, it.

There are a variety of different pronouns that people may use which fall into different categories:

- **Gendered pronouns** – She/her and he/him are gendered pronouns which are used by those who identify as women (she/her) and men (he/him).

- **Nonbinary and gender-neutral pronouns** – They/them are a pronoun set used predominantly by nonbinary individuals and those who identify as a gender which differs from the binary.

Myth: 'They/them pronouns that refer to a singular person are a new thing.' That is so far from the truth it's laughable! 'They/them' pronouns have been used in literature to address a singular person for many years, from as early as the 14th Century. Even Shakespeare, deemed the best poet and playwright of all time, used the singular 'they/them' pronouns in his work – notably in Hamlet. So next time someone says they 'aren't grammatically correct', throw that fact their way and see what they say!

- **Neopronouns** – Neopronouns are a category of third-person personal pronouns beyond 'he', 'she', 'they', 'one' and 'it'. Neopronouns are used by nonbinary people who do not feel a connection to they/them pronouns. There are a variety of neopronouns, with new ones being adopted by the community daily. Here are a few neopronouns:

	Subject Pronouns	Object Pronouns	Possessive Adjectives	Possessive Pronouns	Reflexive Pronouns
They	*They* smiled	I emailed *them*	*Their* hair shines	It is *theirs*	They love *themselves*
Ne	*Ne* smiled	I emailed *nem*	*Nir* hair shines	It is *nirs*	Ne love *nemself*
Ve	*Ve* smiled	I emailed *ver*	*Vis* hair shines	It is *vis*	Ve love *verself*
Spivak	*Ey* smiled	I emailed *em*	*Eir* hair shines	It is *eirs*	Ey love *emself*
Ze/zie and hir	*Ze* smiled	I emailed *hir*	*Hir* hair shines	It is *hirs*	Ze love *hirself*
Ze/zie and zir	*Ze* smiled	I emailed *zir*	*Zir* hair shines	It is *zirs*	Ze love *zirself*
Xe	*Xe* smiled	I emailed *xem*	*Xyr* hair shines	It is *xyrs*	Xe love *xemself*

No pronouns – no problem!

What about those people who do not use *any* pronouns? There are a few different ways these people identify:

- ⊙ **Nullpronominal** – Nullpronominal, voidpronoun, pronounless are all terms for the act of not using third person pronouns.

- ⊙ **Demipronominal** – Demipronominal is the act of using pronouns sometimes, but mostly using no pronouns. This could also be called pronounfluid.
- ⊙ **Nameself** – Some people use their name or nickname in the place of pronouns, this is called nameself.
  Example: 'Zac's favourite sport is football; Zac's position is defender.'
- ⊙ **Emojiself** – Emojiself is the act of using emojis, letters or pictures in the place of pronouns. This is typically only ever written and isn't a pronoun used verbally.
  Example: Instagram Bio: Em (☆/☆☆)
- ⊙ **Nounself** – Nounself is the act of using nouns in the place of pronouns. The nouns used may be gender-related concepts, or not. They could be related to nature, technology, colour, abstract concepts etc.
  Example: 'I love making Hannah laugh, blue has such a hearty laugh!'

'But how can someone use a noun to describe themselves? It doesn't make any sense!'

It may not make sense to you, but, and I don't mean to be rude here, it doesn't matter what you think or feel! If the individual using the nouns to describe themselves feels affirmed when using them, it really doesn't matter what others think!

You may also see some folks who have 'any pronoun' in their bio or will say they don't mind what pronouns you use for them. These people may identify as apathetic gender, someone who doesn't really 'care' how others perceive them or refer to them.

Multiple pronouns

There are many layers to our identities, and even within these layers, there are more layers – we are almost like onions, with each layer unveiling another part that makes us who we are. So, it would make sense that someone may not be able to fully encapsulate themselves in only one set of pronouns and may use more than one set of pronouns that best reflect who they are.

Example:

> Noah is genderfluid and uses both 'he/him' and 'she/her' pronouns depending on how he is feeling or expressing himself on a specific day. In his Instagram bio (which we will get into in a second), Noah has 'he/she', showing people that she uses both pronouns interchangeably.

See how easy it was to use both Noah's pronouns?

Some people who use multiple pronouns may prefer one pronoun over another depending on a variety of factors – how they are feeling on a specific day, what gender identity they feel most closely aligned with, or simply what pronoun they like more!... but how will you know this? It is common practice by multiple pronoun users to put their preferred or favourite pronoun first, so for example, if Noah preferred being called 'he/him' over 'she/her', he would put 'he' in front of 'she' in his bio or use 'he' first when introducing himself. However, not everyone will follow this 'rule' and it's always best to ask the person how they want to be referred to (when it's appropriate to do so).

How many pronouns can someone use? Well, that is truly down to the person and there isn't a limit on how many pronouns a person can use.

Examples:

Ann they/he – Marcus he/ze/em – Alexander ♡/❦/they/he/she

How do you find out what pronouns someone uses?

The best way to find out how best to address someone is to offer your own pronouns first. For example, 'Hey, my name is Joe, my pronouns are "they/them"', or by asking the person what pronouns they use. Some people also use pronoun signifiers, such as a pronoun badge, to tell people what pronouns they use.

How and when do I share my pronouns?

First, why do we need to share our pronouns with anyone? Well, sharing your pronouns with people ensures that they use the correct ones when referring to you, but also shows your allyship to those who use pronouns that aren't the ones they were assigned at birth. Everyone, and I mean *everyone*, benefits from sharing their pronouns with people.

But there are some folks who may not be able or ready to share their pronouns, maybe it's not safe for them to do so, maybe they are still figuring themselves out, or maybe they simply don't want to share their pronouns with people, and it's important that no individual feels pressured to share their pronouns.

There are a variety of ways that we share our pronouns with others, whether that's digitally or in-person, so let's break it down:

DIGITAL

On most apps you can simply add your pronouns in your bio or there will be a designated space for you to input them. Some folks, like me, like to add their pronouns to their names or handles too or in the corner of posts or videos.

EMAILS

You can add a signature onto the end of your emails which will show your name, phone number, social media links and pronouns. This signature will appear on all your emails.

WHAT ABOUT IN PERSON?

Sharing your pronouns in person, some may say, is an art form. Knowing when best to share and not to share can be very important for your own safety, but here's my advice for sharing pronouns in person as someone who does it a lot!

- ◉ Introducing yourself: whenever I meet someone new and share my name, I immediately also share my pronouns afterwards. This nearly always prompts the person I'm speaking to to share their pronouns too.

- ◉ Wearing a pronoun badge: sometimes I will sport a badge which has my pronouns on which can act as a non-verbal signal to others of what pronouns I go by but can also be a good reminder for those whom I have just met or are having trouble remembering my pronouns. Though I wouldn't wear this badge in spaces I don't feel partially comfortable in as I could end up putting myself in danger.

Should you share someone else's pronouns?

Again, safety must be considered, as well as having consent from the person whose pronouns you are sharing. Someone may be out to you but not out to everyone, which means if you share their pronouns to someone they aren't out to, you are in fact 'outing' them.

WHAT DOES 'OUTING' MEAN?

Being 'out' when we talk about gender and sexuality means that people know how we identify, and we share this information with people. There are varying degrees of being 'out', some folks are just out to their close friends, others to family also, and then some are out to everyone. The act of 'outing' someone is forcing someone to publicly share their identity without their consent – this is wrong.

Before you share someone's pronouns, make sure you:

- have consent from the person to share their pronouns with others
- check that the environment in which you are sharing these pronouns is safe for a queer and gender-diverse person to be out in.

In conclusion: *we are all onions*, full of many layers or elements which make up our identity. Gender, one of those layers, can be just as complex, full of a variety of combinations and ways of identifying which differ from person to person, day to day, throughout our entire life.

Chapter 2
Beyond Penis and Vagina

We use the term 'sex' when we are talking about our biology, the innie and outie parts of our bodies, and when we are talking about sexual intercourse. This chapter covers the first.

Before we dive in, it's important I remind you all that it's *totally* ok to blush or feel a smidge embarrassed when talking about anything within this chapter. Some of the words in this may take you back to being in school, feeling your face go bright red or concealing a giggle under your school jumper sleeve. Talking about sex, even just saying *sex*, feels naughty and uncomfortable for most people, and that's unfortunately society's fault. Society has conditioned us into believing that sex, both our bodies and the act, is a taboo topic – which is why we feel giggly when talking about certain things, we feel embarrassed and shameful. Sex, and everything about sex, everything within this book, is **not** taboo – it is all part of our experience as human beings.

Society tells us that we shouldn't talk about our bodies to one another. That we should just get on with what we were given and never ask questions about our ins and outs. We all deserve to know about our bodies beyond just what we can visually see or what society tells us about it, we deserve to be curious, to have a good look at what's between our legs, and to see how ours compares to others! So, let's get curious! As we have already said, gender, sexuality and expression are layered, and sex is no different. There aren't only two types of bodies!

Before we get into our bits, we need to talk about what 'biological sex' means. Biological sex, or **assigned sex** as I prefer to say, is assigned or given to us at birth, usually by a doctor or nurse, and this is the information that gets put on our birth certificate. This typically is either 'male' or 'female', but some folks don't fit neatly into these boxes and are intersex. But how does the doctor assign this label to a baby? This comes down to what genitalia the baby has or hasn't got. However, sex isn't as clear cut as two labels and exists on a spectrum. (An ongoing theme for this book!) But it isn't just our bits and bobs that guide doctors to assign us at birth, our hormones and primary sex characteristics play a role too. As well as a penis or a vulva/vagina, we also have reproductive organs which are connected to our genitalia; together these are called our 'primary sex characteristics'. AFAB babies will have a uterus and AMAB babies will have testicles... but guess what, some folks don't have these reproductive organs *or* have reproductive organs that match the opposite assigned sex. (We will come back to this, do not fear!)

You may have heard of people referring to chromones when discriminating against a trans person. Sadly, this is a comment I've seen thrown around too often, but what does this really mean? Well, here's the science-y bit about our assigned sex: chromosomes are tiny, microscopic structures inside the cells within our bodies and their strands contain DNA that are encoded with genes. Now,

I'm no scientist, but to summarize in a way that I understand, chromosomes are almost like an IKEA instruction manual which was written by our parents. This decides what colour eyes and hair we have, or what blood type we are, or how short or tall we will be when we hit puberty. But we also have a set of special chromosomes which determines our biological sex: expertly named, the sex chromosomes. We will come back to conception in Chapter 8, but what you need to know is that the egg (which is from the AFAB body) carries an X chromosome, and the sperm (which is from the AMAB body) carries either an X or a Y chromosome. And when the sperm and the egg meet, they create individuals with XY chromosomes (AMAB) or XX chromosomes (AFAB) or a mixture of chromosomes, XXY, or some chromosomes that are XY and some that are XX (both intersex).

So, the next time someone talks about chromosomes, ask them if they truly know what they have... because chances are they are simply guessing based on what they were assigned as at birth.

XX chromosomes	XY chromosomes
Clitoris	Penis
Labia majora	Scrotum
Ovaries	Testicles

V is for Vulva... and Vagina, but first vulva

Don't worry if you are looking at the words 'vulva' and 'vagina' and feel confused as to why there are two names for this type of genitalia. Most people grow up only knowing one of these words – I didn't know vulva was a word until 2020. The vulva is the outside part of this genitalia type, and the vagina is the tube of muscle between the cervix and the outside body (the part of the body that is used during sexual intercourse and periods). There are also an array of words that people use when describing the vulva and vagina... some of which are loaded with stereotypes against vulva and vagina owners, and others that have been reclaimed as powerful statements for vulva and vagina owners:

- pussy
- minge
- front bottom
- twat
- fanny
- minnie
- c*nt
- poom
- poonai.

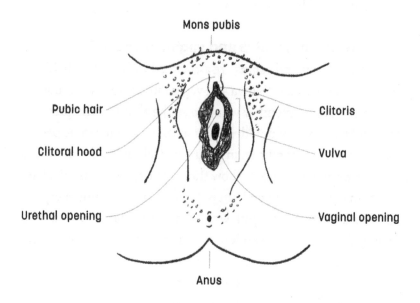

Parts of the vulva also have 'unique' names that people use:

- ⊙ outer labia: flaps/beef curtains/lips
- ⊙ clit: magic button/bean.

The reason some of these words exist is because people feel less embarrassed using them than the actual words for the body parts. But talking about our bodies using the actual terms is not only empowering, allowing ourselves to become familiar with the different parts of our bodies and other bodies, but makes communicating about our bodies easier. Whether it's talking to your doctor or a sexual partner, using the anatomically correct words is key if you can! Talking about our bodies in anatomical terms is also trans inclusive and makes navigating these topics way less dysphoria inducing for gender-diverse individuals like me. But if you want to call it a pussy or a c*nt, go for it!

Why am I saying 'vulva and vagina owners'?

Though the vulva and vagina are associated with AFAB individuals, not everyone who has a vulva and vagina identifies as a woman or was born AFAB. Remember what we spoke about in the previous chapter? Each part of our identity is separate, and for some people their gender is different from their sex. Calling someone with a vagina a woman may not be how they identify. For example, I am a nonbinary vulva owner; I am not a woman. Also, not everyone who has a vulva and vagina was born AFAB. Trans women who have undergone lower gender-affirming surgery will have a constructed vulva and vagina.

There are three options for lower gender-affirming surgery for trans women: orchidectomy which removes the testes; vaginoplasty which removes the penis, testicles and scrotum creating a vaginal canal and labia; and vulvoplasty which creates a vulva, including a mons pubis, labia, clitoris and urethral opening. Trans women and gender-diverse+ folks who have lower gender-affirming surgery can have sex and orgasm – so yeah, it isn't only cis women who have vaginas!

Labia – the other kinds of lips
The labia are folds of skin around the vaginal opening, but there are actually two labias:

- ◎ **The labia minora** are thinner lips which are more flexible. These are the lips that fill with blood and become thicker when aroused.
- ◎ **The labia majora** are the outer lips.

Labia can come in all shapes and sizes, long or short, wrinkled or smooth. They can also vary in colour from a pink to a brownish black, and even more interesting, the colour of your labia may change as you grow older. Some folks have larger outer lips, others have larger inner lips.*

The clitoral hood
The labia minora come together at the top of the vulva to form the clitoral hood, and this is where you will find the clitoris – the star of the show.

---

* I am an 'outie', meaning my inner lips stick out quite a bit and for a long time I HATED this. At one time, I even considered surgery to shorten my lips – but since understanding that this is just how my vulva looks, I have come to love my outie! Being intimate with other vulva owners has also made me realize how beautiful and varying our vulvas are.

C is for Clitoris

First things first, no, the clit isn't hard to find, but many individuals who have a clit haven't even seen theirs, so let's not poke fun at those who don't have one!

The clitoris is a wonderfully underrated part of the body which the sex-positive community have only recently been giving it the platform it deserves. The clitoris has a very important job – pleasure! It is the only organ in the body that is solely for pleasure. It can be touched, licked, sucked, tapped and buzzed with a toy... but we will come back to that in the next chapter. The clitoris is much bigger than most people think it is, and that's because only a small part of it is external – like a beautiful iceberg.

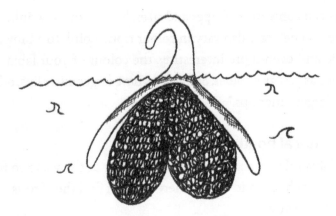

The clitoris is around 10cm in length, the size of a credit card, but this varies from body to body. The part of the clit that is external is often partially or completely covered by the clitoral hood, which protects it as the clit can be super sensitive due to its 10,000 nerve endings! If the clit is responsible for pleasure, then what's the g-spot? It's believed that the g-spot is the internal part of the clitoris being stimulated. Like a lot of the AFAB anatomy and experience, the clitoris has sadly been neglected in the world of science. The clitoris was discovered in 1556 by Renaldus Columbus, but its complete structural discovery happened in 1998 thanks to Helen O'Connell – that's only one year before I was born!! It was in 2005 that we received MRI images of living, aroused clitorises and learnt that it was ten times bigger than most people previously believed it to be. It was only in 2022 that we discovered that the clit had 2000 more nerve endings than we previously thought – double that of the tip of a penis (not to brag).

Arousal

So, what does an aroused clitoris look like? Well... the clit can get hard, much like a penis!

When an individual with a clitoris is turned on, blood rushes to the clit, causing it to swell and become erect/hard. This blood flow may also cause the clitoris and the other external parts of the vulva to become a deeper colour – how cool is that!

It's here that we need to talk about squirting. As an AFAB individual, I am fascinated by those who can squirt because I simply cannot. A 'vulval ejaculation', commonly called squirting, is when fluid leaves the vagina when climaxing. You'll see a lot of conversation online about whether 'squirt is pee' or not, but research suggests that the clear, milky fluid is released from the Skene glands (which we will cover in two seconds!). Squirting is a sign of pleasure, regardless of what the fluid is made of, and it's important to remember that not everyone will be able to squirt. You squirting doesn't equal whether or not you've climaxed or enjoyed sex!

Glands, get your glands here!

Bartholin glands
There are two Bartholin glands below the skin near the vagina which produce fluid that helps keep parts of the vulva moist.

Skene glands
On either side of the urethra, you will find two Skene glands. These glands help to keep the surrounding part of the vulva moist (like the Bartholin glands). This is what makes folks 'wet' when they are aroused.

Now for the other V

Let's talk about the other V – the vagina.

The vagina is a tube which connects the outside of the body to the womb or uterus. Though on the illustration above it may look like the vagina is hollow, in fact the walls typically touch one another (meaning there isn't really that gap in the middle). The vagina is made of very stretchy muscle, which comes in handy when giving birth.

The urethra
For girls, women and AFAB individuals, the pee does not come out of the vagina, it comes out of a hole just above called the urethra which is connected to the bladder, where the pee is stored. This hole is much smaller than the vaginal entrance.

Mons pubis
The mons is the 'fleshy mound' above your vulva, and it is here

where hair grows during puberty...
we will come to body hair soon!

The hymen

Myth: 'You will pop your
cherry after having sex for
the first time.'

Let's talk about the hymen, or
what you may know it to be called
– the 'cherry'. The cherry, which has
the anatomical name hymen, is another
misunderstood part of the AFAB body. The hymen is a thin tissue
covering the vaginal opening. Many believe (incorrectly) that the
hymen rips when having sex for the first time, aka 'popping the
cherry'. Throughout history it is thought that someone who has
an 'intact' hymen is a 'virgin' and you'll know this as they will
bleed during sex. We will come back to the term virgin later.

This isn't true. Some folks' hymens cover most of their vagina
opening; some folks barely have any tissue at all. Some folks are
even born without a hymen! There are a variety of ways that the
hymen tissue may thin out: through sports, biking, horseback rid-
ing, masturbating, using tampons. All of which are *totally* normal
ways of your hymen thinning out. No one can tell if someone
has had sex for the first time by whether they have hymen tissue
– not even a gynaecologist (whose job it is is to look at vulvas and
vaginas!).

Some folks bleed during sex regardless of whether it's their
first time or not, bleeding doesn't indicate someone's first time

and it is *not* a requirement for your first time. Unfortunately, many folks have their hymens 'checked' by medical professionals – this is also called virginity checking – and this is incredibly invasive, inappropriate, unethical and simply wrong in every way. In the UK, these sorts of tests are illegal, but sadly that isn't a global law.

So, there is no cherry to pop... sorry!

The womb and ovaries

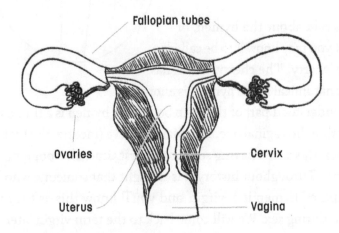

Fallopian tubes

Ovaries

Uterus

Cervix

Vagina

As we've learnt, the vagina connects the outside of the body to the inside, and that 'inside' is called the womb. The womb is a space where a baby would grow if an individual was pregnant. On either side of the womb are the ovaries; it is here that eggs are released from.

Eggs? Yes, egg cells are reproductive cells, and when fused together with a sperm cell (from a man or penis owner), a baby is made. Tah-dah. You might be wondering how this cycle actually works. There's so much to say about periods, I've dedicated the whole of the next chapter to it.

Are they meant to... smell?

Vaginas do not smell of roses or whatever fragrance candle companies are trying to convince you of. Sometimes genitals smell, sometimes they don't, sometimes the smell is barely there and sometimes it is *intense*. Genitals smell because of sweat, discharge, sexual fluids, sex, urine and periods, and you will know your own smell, depending on what you're currently experiencing. This also means you'll notice when your smell doesn't smell right for you – which is when you can get it checked out.

Never wash inside your vagina

Ok, let's get into this – you should *not* be washing inside your vagina, also known as 'douching'. Washing inside your vagina removes helpful bacteria and changes the acidity in the vagina. This can lead to the development of thrush or bacterial vaginosis. There are a lot of products out there that claim to make your vagina smell fruity fresh – vaginal steamers, tablets, sprays, vaginal washes, gels – but many of these can affect your vaginal health. I would personally just avoid them.

Speaking of... what's discharge?

I remember seeing white stuff in my underwear for the first time, I genuinely thought I was dying. Or when I realized my underwear was bleached, I panicked and quickly asked my mum what the heck was going on. Discharge is the vagina's way of cleaning itself, hence why you shouldn't be washing inside your vagina. Some folks, like me, wear liners to protect their underwear or just to feel generally more comfortable. Discharge is 100 per cent normal, but it's important to keep an eye on what colour and consistency your discharge is, as this can let you know if you are healthy or if something is up. So, here's the multi-coloured rainbow of discharge:

- ⦿ **Green or yellow with a bad odour** – it could be a sign of an STI (sexually transmitted infection).
- ⦿ **Clear** – this could be a sign that you're ovulating, how cool.
- ⦿ **Red** – this could mean you're spotting, which happens between periods. Don't worry, this can be totally harmless; however, if you're concerned, do check with your doctor as it may be a sign of a health issue.
- ⦿ **Pink** – can indicate bleeding, infection, irritation or even early pregnancy.
- ⦿ **Grey** – often a sign of infection. If it is also thick and watery, it could be a sign of bacterial vaginosis, which occurs when the balance of bacteria in the vagina is not at its normal levels.

It's like tea-leaf reading... but discharge.

Get to know your vulva and vagina

Knowing your 'normal' when it comes to your vulva and vagina can be lifesaving. Knowing what your body typically looks like, smells like, what your period usually looks like, how it typically feels to pee and have sex is important for knowing when something isn't right. As I said at the beginning of this chapter, being able to just say words and to understand our body can help us to know when to visit a doctor and what to say. Some new usual things you may notice about your bodily functions and genitals may be signs of cancer and it's important that you know what types of gynaecological cancers AFAB folks can get and what they can look like. Please note that I say 'can' because having any of these signs isn't a confirmation; if you do notice any of these signs, book in to see your doctor as soon as you can.

Ovarian cancer – 7000 women and womb owners diagnosed per year in the UK

Ovarian cancer is when abnormal cells in the ovary begin to grow and divide in an uncontrolled way, eventually forming a growth or tumour. If it is not caught early, the cancer cells can grow and spread to other parts of the body.

Symptoms include feeling full quickly, loss of appetite, persistent bloating, pain in your abdomen or lower part of your stomach that doesn't go away, needing to pee more often, change in your bowel habits and movements, unexplained tiredness, weight loss and nausea.

Cervical cancer – most common in cervix owners aged 30–45

Cervical cancer is when abnormal cells in the lining of the cervix grow in an uncontrolled way, forming a growth or tumour. Again, this can grow and spread across the entire body.

Symptoms include unusual vaginal bleeding, pain or discomfort during sex, vaginal discharge, and pain in the pelvis (between the hip bones).

Cervical cancer is the only cancer which has a screening process and programme. Screening means testing people for early stages of a disease or cancer before they have symptoms, but, for this to be useful, tests must be reliable, do better than harm to those taking part and be something folks are willing to do.

However, these tests can be uncomfortable and nerve wracking for some folks and can trigger dysphoria for trans folks for various reasons. One of them being the process itself (which I will deep dive in a moment), or that the language around cervical screenings is still sadly heavily gendered. As a trans AFAB individual, I feel very uncomfortable when seeing my doctor for reproductive health reasons, not only because they used my deadname for over a year until I legally changed it, but because it was very 'woman' and 'female' focused. Everyone with a cervix over the age of 25 needs screening. However, when I received my smear test letter (another phrase used to refer to cervical screenings), the documents they included were super inclusive and used neutral language.

If you're a vagina owner who is trans and have changed your medical record to no longer say 'female', you may not be invited to a screening, so it's important to take your health into your own hands and speak to your doctor to arrange one yourself.

But why over 25? Cervical cancer is rare in AFAB folks under the age of 25, and changes on the cells of the cervix are quite common in this age group. These changes return to normal and are less likely to develop into cancer, meaning screenings can lead to unnecessary treatment and stress.

Let's go back to what the screening itself looks like. Cervical screening, or a smear test, involves a nurse inserting a speculum, a duck-billed shape device, into the vagina to open it and collecting cells from the cervix using a plastic swab. But let's start from the beginning: first the nurse will ask you to remove your clothes from the waist down (yes, that means your underwear) and lie on your back on the patient bed. From here the nurse will give you a paper towel to cover your hip area, will ask you to lift your knees up and spread apart. Then they will insert the speculum. You can ask the nurse to use more lube, or to downsize the speculum, and you can even insert it yourself if that will be more comfortable for you. It's also good to bring a trusted friend or a partner who can take you to your appointment and give you support before and after the procedure.

So, what do these screenings really look for? The screening process tests for a group of 200 related viruses called Human Papilloma Virus, also known as HPV, which cause 99 per cent of cervical cancers. HPV is spread through vaginal, anal and oral sex (we will come back to sexually transmitted diseases in Chapter 8). There are two types of HPV: low-risk, which causes no disease, and high-risk, which causes cancer. HPV infection is super common; in fact nearly all sexually active folks are infected with HPV within months to a few years of becoming sexually active, and around half of those are with a high-risk type.

But what does the vaccination do? There is now a vaccination available that helps prevent infection from disease-causing HPV types, preventing HPV-related cancers and cases of genital warts (we will come back to these bad boys later!). The vaccine is estimated to prevent up to 90 per cent of HPV-related cancers and has already begun reducing rates of cervical cancer across the globe.

Womb cancer – 9 out of 10 womb cancers are picked up early because of irregular bleeding

Also called uterine cancer as the uterus is the medical name for the womb, you may also hear it called endometrial cancer.

Symptoms include bleeding after menopause, bleeding that is unusually heavy or happens between periods, and discharge that is pink or watery or dark and foul smelling. However, unusual bleeding isn't only a symptom of womb cancer, it's also a sign of endometriosis, as well as fibroids, endometrial hyperplasia, growths in the womb lining, and uterine bleeding (which is bleeding for no obvious underlying cause). We will discuss this further in Chapter 3.

Vaginal cancer – 20 in 100 women and vagina owners who are diagnosed with vaginal cancer have no symptoms at all

Possible symptoms include bleeding between periods or after menopause, or after sex, discharge that smells or is blood stained, pain during penetration, a lump or growth in the vagina or vaginal itching.

Vulval cancer – again, not everyone with vulval cancer will have symptoms

Possible symptoms include an open sore or growth which is visible on the skin, a non-stop itch, bleeding, pain or soreness, a mole which changes shape or colour, burning pain when you wee or thickened, raised, red, white or dark patches on your skin.

Chest

Does the size of your chest matter?

When it comes to your chest or breasts, the size does not matter one single bit! Whether you are part of the itty-bitty titty committee (aka have a smaller chest) or have a larger chest, your chest is unique to you and is valid! Typically, your chest will start to develop around the age of 9 to 11, but some folks develop their chest much earlier than others, and some develop much later in their teen years. Some folks wear a bra or sports bra to support their chest, some can go bra-less or wear a bralette that has less support. Some folks bind their chest to appear flatter, and I don't just mean trans folks – some cisgender girls and women also bind daily. Folks also worry about the size and shape of their nipples – but again, these come in all kinds of shapes and shades! Some with hair, some without. Some folks get theirs pierced and others find their nipples super sensitive. The areola (the outer circle around your nipple) and the nipple itself can range from a baby pink to a muddy brown to black. Some are inverted, meaning they do not protrude outwards, some are completely flat to the chest and others noticeably stick out. And that's not all, your nipples also change throughout your life or depending on your mood. When you're aroused or cold or being touched, they get hard. Nipples are pretty neat!

The size of your chest has zero to do with anyone else but you – some folks who have a larger chest may seek breast reduction later in life to help reduce back pain, some folks who have a smaller chest may want a boob job, and others may want top surgery (removing your breasts for a flatter look). Regardless, as long as you're happy with your chest, and it's healthy, then that's all that matters!

Get to know your chest

Talking about a healthy chest, it's vital that you check your chest on a regular basis. Again, it's key to know your own 'normal' and that means getting touchy with your chest. It's also good to know how your chest changes during your cycle, again to know your own normal rhythm.*

---

* See https://coppafeel.org/breast-cancer-info-and-advice/how-do-i-check

Before we get into how you check your chest (which is also important for AMAB folks to know), I want to say that it isn't easy for everyone. I have a love-hate relationship with my chest and have done ever since I started developing. A lot of trans AFAB folks dislike their chest, which can make checking it difficult and dysphoric – I struggle touching my chest when I'm feeling dysphoric, so I make sure that when I'm feeling good about my body and chest, I check myself all over, mostly in the shower.

- ⊙ **Look** – Look for any changes in skin texture and swelling in your armpit or around your collar bone. Keep an eye out for discharge, sudden changes in size or shape or colour, as well as nipple inversion or change in direction.
- ⊙ **Feel** – Feel around for lumps. Also take note if you feel a constant, unusual pain in your breast or armpit.

If in doubt, get it checked out! Your doctor can refer you for further examination if you're unsure of what you feel. You can also ask for a doctor of the same gender, or for a chaperone if this will make it easier for you (particularly for trans folks!).

P is for Penis

Much like the vulva and vagina, the penis has an array of words that people use for it and for the parts of it; here are just some you may have heard of before:

- ⊙ dick
- ⊙ willy
- ⊙ ding-dong

- ⊙ head (bell end)
- ⊙ member
- ⊙ schlong.

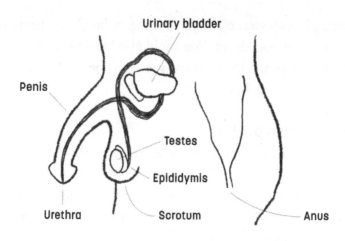

Let's get hard: What is an erection?

Erection is the rigid state of a penis, which causes it to point away from the body, which occurs when the spongy tissue inside the penis fills with blood – this is also called 'getting hard' or 'having a boner'. The penis becomes erect/hard so that it can be used to penetrate or masturbate and is typically triggered by arousal.

Some erections are caused by arousal, but many are completely random, with no trigger whatsoever, happening in not the best of places. You can even wake up with an erection! In summary, erections aren't something you can control, especially when you are going through puberty; erections can simply sneak attack you out of nowhere – but it's important to remember, this is totally normal and most people with a penis have experienced an unexpected erection. Some folks may also get 'semis' and this means they are half-way towards having a boner, but aren't 100 per cent there yet, and again this can happen for no reason at all.

Can you hide an erection? Yes and no. If you can, try to sit down somewhere, you can hide it between your legs. Or try covering it with your clothing, or a bag, or bend over to tie your shoe whilst it goes down. You could also head to the bathroom until it disappears. Don't worry, you won't be the first to try to hide a 'boner' in public!

People with a penis?

Yes, it isn't only men and boys who have a penis – trans women, nonbinary folks and gender-diverse people may also have a penis... and they too may have difficulties with erections throughout their lives. And just as we discussed about vaginas, not everyone with a penis was born with one!

There are several gender-affirming procedures for trans men and those wanting a penis. One is the construction of a penis, also called phalloplasty, which involves using a flap of skin, typically from the forearm or thigh area, to create a larger neophallus. Metoidioplasty creates a micropenis by bringing the clitoris forward. There is also the construction of a scrotum, called scrotoplasty, and testicular implants and penile implants. There are also simpler surgeries for those who have experienced bottom growth,* but we will explore those when we discuss 'second puberty' later.

Not only are surprise erections a possibility, but you may also have difficulties with staying erect or getting erect throughout your life. It can be tough during sex (which includes masturbation) to get or stay hard for a variety of reasons including tiredness, stress, being intoxicated with drink or drugs, medication, illness, mental health or the anxiety of performing. However, struggling to get hard or stay hard is a totally normal thing that happens to

---

* Bottom growth is the process of clitoral hypertrophy, or the clitoris growing in length and width while taking testosterone.

most penis owners, several times throughout their life. However, if you're struggling to get/stay erect on a regular basis and if it's impacting your sex life, then speaking to your doctor is vital because you may have erectile dysfunction.

Some people have foreskin, some don't, some have too much!

Foreskin is the fold of skin that covers the head of a flaccid (not hard) penis. When the penis gets hard, the foreskin moves back, meaning the head of the penis is exposed. However, some folks have foreskin long enough to cover the head of their penis even when they are hard.

Why remove it? Some folks have their foreskin removed as babies; this is called circumcision and there's typically only two reasons for this: religious or cultural reasons (it's common practice in Jewish and Islamic communities), or medical reasons (conditions such as a tight foreskin, known as phimosis). Yes, some folks may find that they have a tight foreskin, which doesn't easily roll back over the head of the penis when they are erect. Tight foreskin isn't an issue, unless it causes symptoms such as redness, swelling, discharge and inflammation of the head of the penis, in which case contact your doctor.

Does size matter?

The average size of a penis (whilst hard) is 5.1 inches in length – the size of most phones or teaspoons. But the 'average category' for the length of a penis varies and includes penises of 3–4 inches too. Though I hate saying 'average' as many folks worry that that is code for 'normal' – it isn't! Penises come in a variety of sizes and girths.

But you have probably heard a joke or two about someone's

penis size. 'Dick' and all its synonyms can also be used as an insult towards someone who is being annoying, to put it lightly. 'Dick' and dick jokes are unfortunately part of our vocabulary; you've most likely called someone a dick before, or laughed at a penis joke, or even made your own joke towards someone – we are all guilty of it. We are wayyy more comfortable using 'dick' or 'penis' in everyday conversation than we are of saying vagina or vulva... which is interesting don't you think? And sadly, these jokes perpetuate negative stereotypes about penises and penis owners. Jokes about penis size are layered. Not only do these jokes or insults hurt folks and make them feel self-conscious about their genitals, but they can also push racial stereotypes, particularly towards cis Black and Asian men (the stereotype that Black men always have larger penises whilst Asian men have smaller penises).

Some folks believe that the bigger the penis, the better the sex, but this isn't always the case. There is so much more to sex than penis size, which we will explore shortly.

Small dick jokes impact people across a variety of identities, not only cisgender men. Smaller penises are commonly found among trans men or gender-diverse folks who are taking testosterone (we will come back to trans bodies in a moment). Their penises are just as valid regardless of their size. Some naturally smaller penises, also known as 'micropenises', are considered an intersex variation. Again, genitals exist on a spectrum and there are a variety of different genital types and sizes. Folks with a 'larger clit' or a 'smaller penis' might actually fall into the intersex category, which makes jokes about smaller penises an example of *interphobia* (prejudice or discrimination towards folks who are intersex).

Cleaning your peen

To clean, or not to clean... is *not* the question. You must clean your penis in the shower or bath every day with warm water. But how do you clean your penis? Now that *is* the question!

Maintaining good hygiene and care of your penis will reduce the chance of developing skin irritations and common infections and will keep it smelling a-ok! Yes – when you do not wash your penis it will become smelly, and a layer of white discharge will build under the foreskin. This discharge is called smegma, but you may know of it by its more casual name 'dick cheese'. Did I ever think I would be writing the phrase 'dick cheese' in a book of mine before? No, but life takes you on wild journeys! Anyway – it's important to keep your peen clean to avoid this cheesy build-up.

⊙ Carefully pull back and clean underneath your foreskin, as well as the tip of your penis, with warm water and a very gentle soap (do not use fragrances, keep your spa mild and unperfumed!).

⊙ Use only a small amount of soap; too much can cause irritation.

⊙ When drying your penis, gently pat the tip dry, as well as the area underneath the foreskin and around. Make sure your foreskin is covering the tip of your penis before putting your underwear on.

⊙ Make sure your underwear is clean and fully dried before putting it on.

⊙ Do not use fragrances, oils, lotions or talc on your penis and the rest of your genital area.

E is for Ejaculation

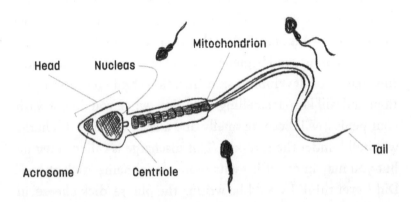

You most likely have heard of ejaculation's more casual name, 'cumming'. Ejaculation, or cumming, happens when an individual reaches orgasm; at this point semen passes through the urethra. Unlike AFAB folks, urine and semen passes through the same hole for AMAB folks, through the tip of the penis (no, you cannot pee and cum at the same time!). Healthy semen is a white-ish, grey-ish colour with a texture similar to raw egg or runny jelly. The average ejaculation produces 1/4 teaspoon to a single teaspoon of semen. Pre-cum is similar in colour and texture; however, as the name implies, it comes out of the individual's penis prior to an orgasm. Pre-cum still can get someone pregnant as it contains sperm – we will come back those little swimmers in Chapter 8! An erection will go away on its own after ejaculation; the penis will become soft and flaccid again.

You know how I said you can have an erection in your sleep? Well, penis owners can also ejaculate in their sleep. This is called a 'wet dream'. However, it isn't only penis owners who have wet dreams, women and AFAB individuals can too!

WET DREAMS ARE MADE OF THIS!

What are wet dreams? Its official name is 'nocturnal emission', and it is when a person has an orgasm in their sleep, which may result in ejaculation, hence the 'wet' part. A wet dream can happen for a variety of reasons, but most come with a very sexy dream and touching of the self while the person is asleep, though some folks can ejaculate without touching themselves whilst asleep or become wet. Sometimes a wet dream just happens... and sometimes in the worst situations. I've only ever had a handful of wet dreams and there's nothing embarrassing about having them, especially if you're a young individual going through puberty or a trans person going through second puberty. But also, not everyone has wet dreams; some may have a few and others may never have one.

Oh no, I've dropped my balls...

When we say balls, we mean testicles – you may also have heard them being called crown jewels, nuts, bollocks, rocks and various other names. Testicles 'drop', meaning they descend into the scrotum, usually within six months of being born, but some folks may 'drop' later in life than others. Don't worry, you won't be dragging your balls across the floor, they will only drop a slight amount, though some may drop more than others. It's also totally natural for one to drop slightly lower than the other one and it prevents them from hitting one another.

Testicles have a very important role. They produce sperm, billions of sperm throughout an individual's lifetime. For sperm to be produced, the testicles need to be at the right temperature, so they will drop or rise depending on how hot or cold you are to create the perfect habitat for sperm – that's pretty neat in my opinion!

Get to know your penis and testicles!

No one should know your body better than you – and that means you've got to touch and look at it. Knowing what your body typically looks and feels like, what 'normal' means to you, allows you to know when something isn't right and that can make a huge difference for seeking care and/or treatment.

When it comes to your genitals, it's vital that you are examining your testicles regularly, and don't worry, it's super easy and should become part of your washing routine. Every few weeks, when you shower, cup your scrotum in the palm of your hand and use your fingers and thumb to look at and feel each testicle. Typically, testicles are smooth and firm, but not hard, and do not have lumps. This is where it's important to know your normal – check for any new or unusual lumps, swelling changes in size or shape or colour and check the differences between the two testicles. As always, if you notice anything 'unusual', speak with your doctor as soon as possible.

Your partner will also know your 'normal' if you've been with them long-term and you've been intimate. If you ever notice something on your partner, it's always a good idea to check in with them to see if they know and to provide support if they don't. I've had partners point out things to me down below that I didn't know were there, which I've then checked out! There's nothing embarrassing about it, you're just looking out for your partner's sexual wellbeing – it's cute in my books!

Cancer in men and those with a penis

I know it's a scary subject, but we have to talk about cancer to best know how to spot the signs.

TESTICULAR CANCER

Testicular cancer mostly affects those between ages 15 and 49, making it more unusual and less common than other forms of cancer. It typically causes changes to the testicles or scrotum, including swelling which is painless, lumps, a change to firmness or texture, or a dull or sharp pain which comes and goes. Knowing how your testicles typically feel and look will help you to spot when things aren't as 'normal' for you – so make sure to touch your balls! If you notice any changes, check in with your doctor.

PROSTATE CANCER

Prostate cancer affects men and those assigned male at birth aged over 40 and is the fourth most common cancer overall. Folks with the male reproductive system have prostate glands which are the size of a walnut, found underneath the bladder, surrounding the urethra. As an individual grows, the size of these grow and can sometimes become enlarged. Those above the age of 40 should ask for a screening test to find early signs of prostate cancer because most folks in the early stages don't have any symptoms. However, things you may notice include changes in your pee, back, hip or pelvic pain, blood in your pee or semen, and unexplained weight loss. If you notice any of these, it's good to check in with your doctor. If you're under the age of 40 it's unlikely that these symptoms may be early signs of prostate cancer, but it's always good to still get checked.

PENILE CANCER

Penile cancer is extremely rare, affecting those aged over 50 years old, and there are a few different types of this particular cancer.

Signs of penile cancer include growths and sores on the penis which don't seem to go away, bleeding, discharge from the penis or under the foreskin, a change in the colour of the skin, a rash and difficulty pulling the foreskin back. Again, if you experience any of these, it's always good to check in with your doctor, even if they turn out to be nothing.

All about puberty

Now that we have a good understanding of our body parts, what they are called, what they can do, let's talk about the dreaded puberty. Yes, puberty can be a difficult time for most folks – but it gets a lot of bad rep for something so natural that happens to most folks around the world. Even if you've been in the trenches of puberty, you may not know that some of the things you experienced were because of this change, or that they can continue way into adulthood. We've already touched on the wonders of periods, wet dreams, erections, but we have missed out on some of the most fun parts of puberty... said no one *ever*!

First – what is puberty?

Puberty is when you transition from childhood to adulthood, both with your body and mind, and no, we will not be using terms like 'womanhood' or 'manhood' here. These changes within our bodies typically occur between the ages of 8 and 14, but say it with me folks: everyone is unique. Some folks may experience puberty earlier than others; I began the beautiful awkward journey of puberty at age seven when acne decided to find a home on my cheeks and shoulder blades. Trans folks may also go through a second puberty when they begin to medically transition, and some folks go through puberty at a much later age, so knowing what happens during puberty is important at all ages!

Acne

Me and acne go wayyy back, we've had an on and off again relationship since I was seven and she just couldn't stay away for too long. Acne is totally and utterly normal, and most folks will get a pimple or two throughout their life... but some of us get a lot of them in one go. Most folks who have regular acne can manage it with a good skincare routine (and, no, this isn't just for the girlies; everyone deserves a good skincare routine) and applying acne products. Though it is important to also allow your natural oils to do their thing and to not dry your skin out by overapplying acne creams. If you're someone like me who has had acne for a very long time, you've probably cycled through most products and had to ask your doctor for more heavy-duty creams – I have tried every single product that my doctor could provide me.

A pro-tip: *Do not* pop, squeeze, scratch or pick your spots. You'll risk an infection, spreading the acne or even scarring.

Do I smell?

If you've ever been near the boys' changing room in school, you'll know that puberty can affect your smell and sweat levels, but it isn't just AMAB folks who get smelly during puberty. We all get smelly during puberty because our sweat glands under our arms and legs become more active – and for some of us, we need to adapt our cleaning routine to defeat these new smells (which doesn't come easy to a lot of us!).

Why am I so hairy??

Hair grows under your armpits, around your genitals (called pubic hair) and possibly on your arms, legs, belly, chest, nipples and face. Not only will new hair grow, but your original hair may become darker and greasier. For some folks, this hair growth takes longer than others, and some folks never grow hair in certain areas or struggle to. I think we have all seen an AMAB individual who can't grow a full beard and has patches (and that is nothing to be embarrassed about!). But what is the purpose of pubic hair? Why is it there? Well, here's some theories: it helps maintain the optimal temperature of the pubic region, it protects the genital area, or that it indicates a biological readiness for reproduction (which just sounds yuck to me). However, the reality is, pubic hair is just there and it's up to you what you do with it. And yes, there is also hair around the anus, which again is totally normal and also up to you what you do with it!

To shave, or not to shave? That is another fun question – it's completely up to you and only you can make that decision, sorry! Weirdly society tries to tell us how we should wear our hair, whether we should grow it out or shave it all off. And even weirder yet is that what is in trend changes. In Ancient Rome, the removal of pubic hair was a status symbol, whilst in Europe until the late 1900s, pubic hair was in fashion. Then in 1987, the first waxing salon opened in America and offered the 'Brazilian wax'. During the height of the pandemic, AFAB folks decided to let their hair grow and it became a mini social movement. I, for one, was one of the folks who stopped shaving during the pandemic.

Having body hair is 100 per cent natural and something you should never be ashamed of, and in the same breath, you should never feel ashamed for *not* having hair. People of all genders have hair, don't have hair, shave, laser, grow it long, even bleach and dye it a fun colour (trust me, I've seen someone with bleached neon pink armpit hair before and it was cool) – truly the options are endless! Body hair can also be super gender-affirming for trans folks, including myself. Rocking hairy legs was one of the first steps on my gender journey, and for many folks, either letting your hair grow out or keeping it clean and tidy can feel euphoric. Trans AMAB folks may choose to undergo laser removal to help keep a clean and hairless look on their face and jaw line, practically if they want a more feminine look, whilst trans AFAB may choose to undergo hormone replacement therapy (which we will cover shortly) which can increase hair growth across the entire body. Some nonbinary and gender-diverse folks may have hair one day but not the next – it really is down to personal preference and what feels good to you.

For some folks who are autistic, body hair can trigger sensory overload (overstimulation due to your five senses taking in more information than your brain can process), which can mean having hair or removing hair is too stimulating and even unbearable for some. I cannot stand armpit hair in its growing out stage, it's so prickly, gets caught on my sleeves and generally hurts, which is why I prefer to keep it longer.

Anything else?

Other changes include growing pains in your arms and legs, a deeper voice (for both AMAB and AFAB folks) and Adam's apple (laryngeal prominence) for AMAB folks, mood swings including anger, anxiety, depression, stress and, finally, sexual thoughts. And that's the joys of puberty.

Trans bodies

Some transgender and nonbinary folks choose to undergo hormone therapy, to better align their body with how they identify.

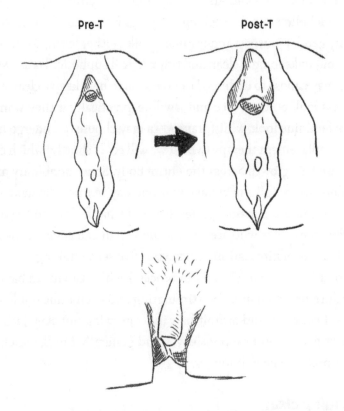

Pre-T   Post-T

AFAB genital changes on testosterone HRT

Before we jump in, it's important that I say that folks can only access hormonal therapy from the age of 16, and those who do must have been on hormone blockers for at least a year prior to commencing them (in the UK at least).

Some trans folks say that they go through a 'second puberty' when undergoing hormone replacement therapy (HRT). This is because their body changes to align more with the gender identity they wish to become closer to.

For AFAB folks who undergo testosterone HRT, they may experience bottom growth, which is when the clitoris grows in length and width. This growth varies from person to person. Sadly, we do not have much clinical information on bottom growth, but we do have insight from those who have undergone HRT. Typically, folks experience around 1 to 4cm of growth, with some noticing the changes within 3–6 months while others only notice it a year to three years into their treatment. And some folks don't experience much change at all.

This growth can feel very sensitive, with some AFAB folks describing it as slightly painful, itchy and almost like a pressure, though most say the discomfort eases within six months of treatment. Even walking can cause some discomfort. To combat this, trans folks taking testosterone (T) may try different types of underwear to find a brand or design that doesn't irritate them. Some also use lube to ease the discomfort.

WHAT IF YOU DON'T WANT BOTTOM GROWTH?

If you don't want to experience intense bottom growth as a trans AFAB individual, you can potentially adjust the T dosage. The lower the dosage, the less likely the effects will be as intense or sudden. Some folks also take finasteride or dutasteride to keep bottom growth minimal – either way, you should talk with your doctor and express these feelings either prior to starting T or during your journey.

IS IT REVERSIBLE?

The standard advice is that, no, it's not reversible once the growth starts. However, as I said, we don't know too much about bottom growth and some trans folks have said their growth did revert if they were on a very low dosage or weren't on the dosage for long. Either way, it's important to talk with your doctor prior about this if it is a concern of yours.

SURGERY FOR BOTTOM GROWTH

There are a few options for surgery on bottom growth to enhance the length. All involve clitoral release, which detaches the clitoris from the pubic bone, allowing it to be moved forward and become more prominent. Alongside clitoral release, there is pubic liposuction, which makes the micropenis look bigger; bulking, which involves using the labia minora to bulk up the micropenis; and finally scrotoplasty, which we have already covered.*

CLEANING YOUR NEW PEEN

Speaking to trans men, they shared that their growth came out of nowhere and having to keep their new peen clean was something they had to learn… but also navigate the hyper-sensitivity of their bottom growth. Some shared that desensitizing themselves to washing their bottom growth was the easiest option, whilst others said that it was just too sensitive, so simply allowing water to run over it was easier. Just as with all penis owners, you need to keep your peen clean and that will involve pulling back your new foreskin.

---

* Amazing resource: https://www.gires.org.uk/wp-content/uploads/2014/08/lower-surgery.pdf

REST OF THE BODY
Other impacts of taking testosterone may include:

- Your voice may break and drop
- You may gain facial hair and hair all over your body
- Increased libido (more on that soon)
- Temperature increase – sweating
- You may notice fat redistribution, with more forming on your tummy and gut
- You may gain muscle
- Change in appetite
- A change in sexual desires (again, more on that soon).

AMAB genital changes on oestrogen HRT

For AMAB individuals who choose to undergo oestrogen HRT, they may experience a decrease in erections and sperm production, with some experiencing erectile dysfunction. They may also find that their testicles shrink to less than half their original size; this typically occurs between three and six months after beginning HRT. However, the amount of skin on the scrotum does not change, meaning there may be excess skin which, if you're considering having bottom surgery, can be used to create a labia majora.

CHEST
Some trans women and gender-diverse+ folks who undergo oestrogen HRT may see breast/chest development. This can be painful for the first few months. Folks can vary in size, but typically will either be an 'A' cup or a small 'B' cup, and sometimes each breast can be slightly different in size. For those wanting to get a

boob job, it's recommended they wait at least a year after starting hormones to see how their chest develops.

REST OF THE BODY
Other bodily changes include:

- Facial hair and body hair grows at a slower rate but unfortunately doesn't stop entirely
- If you are balding, this may slow down or stop entirely
- You may notice a change in foot size or dress size
- Your skin may become softer and less oily
- You may become more prone to bruising or cuts
- You may experience fat redistribution, particularly near your thighs and hips.

Going through a second round of puberty for trans folks can be difficult. It's just as annoying as your first! But for many trans folks, having a body which is closer to how they identify, a body they feel at home in, is all that matters.

Intersex bodies

Intersex is a term used to describe someone whose body isn't categorized by a doctor or nurse as 'male' or 'female'. There are many ways a person can be intersex: some people have internal and/or external genitalia and sex organs that fall outside the binary categories. Other intersex people have a combination of chromosomes that are different from XY (typically associated with male) and XX (typically associated with female). However, intersex people are typically assigned a legal sex of either 'male' or 'female' depending on which one they closely match, such as XXY. Some people may not even know they are intersex until they hit puberty, and some people never know or discover that they are intersex. You could be intersex and have NO clue – how fun! There's estimated to be between 1.7 per cent and 4 per cent of people around the world with intersex conditions, roughly the same number as redhead folks.

An intersex person may choose to identify as the sex they were assigned at birth, but some may identify as a different gender or as trans.

Before we get into the science-y stuff, I want to talk about language. You may have heard of people using the term 'hermaphrodite' when referring to intersex folks; it's also a commonly searched term on porn sites (we will come back to this later). 'Hermaphrodite' is an outdated term implying that a person is both fully male and fully female, functioning in perfect unity (I've heard people say things like 'they have both a vagina and a penis') – however, this isn't biologically possible in humans. Hermaphroditism can occur in the animal kingdom; the starfish for example has both complete reproductive organs which is pretty neat, but this isn't the case in people. Many intersex folks consider the term derogatory and stigmatizing. When we refer to folks who have a variation of sex, we should always use the term 'intersex'.

There are a lot of different ways (roughly 40 of them) that a person may be intersex. Some folks are born with genitalia or reproductive organs (or lack of) that are ambiguous, meaning a doctor can't clearly decide the baby's sex by looking at their genitals when they are born. In fact, around 1 in 1500 babies are born with genitalia that is ambiguous. What does ambiguous genitalia look like? Here are some examples:

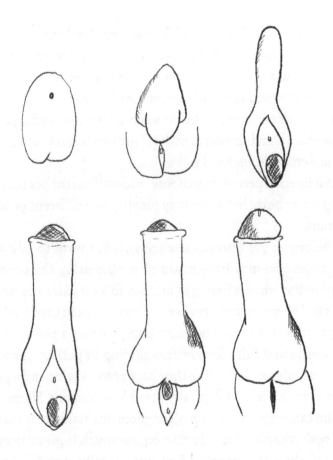

So, what happens in this case? One option is that the child is assigned a binary sex that they fit most closely in on their birth certificate and forced into this binary identity. Folks who are assigned a binary sex at birth may come to find out that they are intersex later in life and with that can come a desire to be seen as their true self legally (changing your legal sex can be super difficult, particularly in countries where intersex recognition is not a thing). Or another option is to carry out surgery to 'fix' a baby's genitalia to align more closely to one binary sex. After this 'correction', the child can then be identified as a binary sex legally. These surgeries often take place before a child is two years old. However, this is extremely controversial and completely unnecessary. Being intersex is completely naturally occurring in humans and isn't a medical issue to solve or fix – it's just a variation of sex. Unfortunately, within the UK there are no laws preventing this at the time of writing this book. Many intersex organizations and activists want parents to let their children choose whether they want surgery or treatment when they are old enough, whilst others believe most surgeries are completely unnecessary.

Another way folks may be intersex is by having different levels of hormones than you'd expect to find in someone assigned the sex that they are. For example, someone who is intersex may have heightened levels of oestrogen but also have a penis, and someone else may have a vulva and vagina but heightened levels of testosterone. Again, this may go completely unnoticed until later in life or at all, but some folks do see the signs of heightened hormone levels that do not match their genitalia, particularly during puberty. Other intersex individuals may have combinations of chromosomes that are different from XX or XY. Some combinations include XXY, XYY, XXX and XXXY. Most folks go through life never knowing if they have a different chromosome combination, unless they have physical differences that may suggest so.

What about puberty? As I've said, some folks find out that they are intersex during puberty and there are a lot of different ways to go through puberty as an intersex individual. Some intersex folks will have a 'typical' puberty whilst others may go through puberty later than their peers, and some may experience some elements of puberty and not others. For example, a 19-year-old girl or AFAB individual may be confused as to why she hasn't had her period yet whilst all her friends have started theirs. Or a boy or AMAB individual may start developing breasts and curvy hips during puberty.

And that's sex! Like the other three elements of what makes us *us*, sex is a spectrum with many different possibilities, and it can be tricky to define neatly into binary boxes. Whether you are trans, intersex, AFAB or AMAB, your sex is valid. Sex is an element of our makeup that can be a little confusing, a little science-y for most (me included), but it's important to understand how our sex impacts us and our everyday life. For all individuals, knowing about how your body works and looks, both internally and externally, means you can seek out medical help sooner rather than later if something doesn't look or feel right. It also makes a rather confusing time, such as puberty, a lot easier – understanding why your body is doing new things can make this time a lot less intimidating.

Chapter 3
Beyond Pads and Tampons

As promised, there's so much to say and understand about periods that I've dedicated a whole chapter to it. Whether you've never had a period or have had many over the years, there's a lot to learn about the menstrual cycle.

'That time of the month'/'red sea'/'on the rag'/'code red' – just say period!

Period isn't a dirty word, or a dirty thing that AFAB people experience. Again, these words exist because people feel uncomfortable or embarrassed saying sex-related words such as period... particularly those who do not have periods. But periods aren't this secret, taboo thing that only a few people experience. Half the population have periods at some point of their life. You've definitely used the bathroom after someone who is on their period. Or sat next to someone who has periods. Or you live with people who menstruate. So let's start using the actual word and learn more about what periods actually are!

Period ≠ woman

Not everyone who menstruates is a woman, and not every woman menstruates! I am a nonbinary person who menstruates. Some women don't have periods. So, menstruation isn't a 'women only' thing and our language must reflect that. Why might someone who has a uterus not have a period you may ask? Well, there's a variety of reasons, both within our control and outside of it, short-term or long-term: they may not have started puberty yet, they may be going through menopause or be postmenopausal, they may be pregnant, they may have had surgery, they may be on contraception that stops their periods, their weight and lifestyle may impact their cycle, their ovaries may not function (amenorrhoea).

How can we refer to people who have periods without saying women? Well, I just used an example, 'people who have periods', but here's some more options:

◉ menstruators
◉ people who bleed
◉ people who menstruate.

So, can I never say 'women'?
No, I'm not saying you can't say 'woman' or 'women' when you're talking about periods, particularly your own experience. Inclusive language means including everyone; so as long as when you talk about periods everyone who has one feels represented, then that's great! For example, you could say 'women and those who menstruate' – this covers everyone who may have a period.

Who can have a period?

- AFAB folks
- Women
- Trans men
- Trans masculine folks

- Nonbinary folks
- Gender-diverse folks
- Intersex folks.

The menstrual cycle

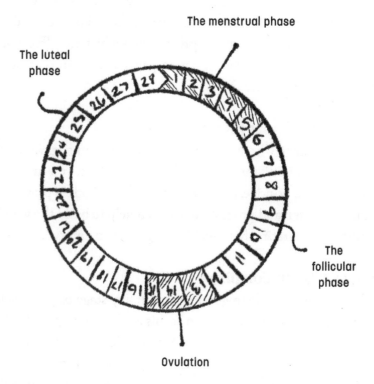

The menstrual phase

The luteal phase

The follicular phase

Ovulation

Stage 1: Menstrual phase

This is the period – aka when you will be bleeding. Of course, this only occurs if an egg hasn't been fertilized during the menstrual cycle. The body discards the uterine lining (also called the endo-metrial tissue), mucus and blood over four to eight days, preparing itself for the cycle to start again. Again, not everyone will bleed over four to eight days – this varies from person to person; my periods are very short compared to most people's, only lasting two to three days (which is a blessing and a curse as they are super heavy!). During these four to eight days, you may experience cramping, back pain, headaches, a sore chest, mood swings, increased hunger bloating and period poops (yes, they are a real thing caused by an increase of compounds called prostaglandins and a decrease of the hormone progesterone which can affect your digestive system... and yes, shooting pains in your anus are also common on your period).

Stage 2: Follicular phase

This is the stage where your body is preparing an egg, which is about 0.1mm in diameter. Throughout this stage, you may feel energized and positive, and that's because your body is providing more oestrogen and progesterone which help to build the womb lining in preparation for a fertilized egg, aka an embryo.

Stage 3: Ovulation phase

Though it is possible to get pregnant at any stage of your cycle, it's more likely during ovulation as this is when an egg is released from your ovaries, ready and raring to be fertilized by a sperm. Sperm can live up to five days in the AFAB reproductive system, providing a lengthy window for the sperm to become friendly with the matured egg. If you are having P in V sex during this period, ensuring you are participating in safer sex practices is vital – we will cover this soon!

During this phase you may experience a mood change, or a loss or increase in appetite, cramps and chest sensitivity.

Final stage: Luteal phase

Once you have finished ovulating, the lining of the womb becomes thick enough for a fertilized egg to implant. But what if there isn't a fertilized egg? Well, in that case the levels of oestrogen and progesterone decrease, which triggers the start of your period. During this stage, you may experience symptoms of PMS (premenstrual syndrome) which can include mood swings, issues sleeping, bloating, weight gain, weird food cravings and chest tenderness.

And then we go through each stage again, and again, and so on. Tah-dah!

How much blood is 'normal'?

Typically, there is about one to five tablespoons' worth of period blood that leaves your body during your period, but it can certainly feel like wayyy more. Some folks, like me, can have very heavy flows, others may have lighter flows, some have light flows at the start of their period and heavy flows near the middle, some may stop bleeding for a few days and then start again – all of which is totally normal.

What period products are available?

There are many period products out there that you can use, and everyone will have their own personal preferences. For example,

BEYOND BANANAS AND CONDOMS

tampons can make some trans folks feel dysphoric, so what options do we have? The first time I used a tampon I fainted, and my mum found me in the bathroom, but I tried a few more times and eventually realized they weren't for me!

Period pads (disposable)

Period pads which are disposable are strips of padding that have a sticky side that you attach to your underwear. The other side, which directly touches your skin, is made of an absorbent material that soaks up the blood.

Period pads are typically a menstruator's first choice when they begin their periods as they are super easy to use! Period pads come in a variety of thicknesses and sizes which can be used by a variety of bodies or at different stages of your period. Pads should be changed around every four to six hours, depending on your flow, but can be changed more frequently if necessary. You can't flush pads down the toilet, you must dispose of them in a bin.

Period pads (reusable)

Reusable pads are just like disposable ones, used in the same manner. The only difference is that these are made from fabric (cloth), that can be washed and reused.

Menstrual cups

Menstrual cups are made from medical-grade silicone, coming in a variety of different colours, and are around two inches in size. Menstrual cups are inserted inside the vagina and collect blood rather than absorbing it. Don't worry, the cup won't fall out – the cup stays inside the vagina due to suction, which is why, when you remove it, you must break the suction seal. When you have removed the cup, you can tip the blood into the toilet, wash it and reinsert it. It's best to follow the instructions on your personal menstrual cup on how to insert and remove it. Menstrual cups are reusable and environmentally friendly and can be cheaper in the long-term!

Period underwear/boxers

Period pants are designed to be worn like everyday underwear, but they absorb period blood like other period products and are reusable. You'll need a few pairs of period underwear as you will need to wash each pair after each day. Again, read the washing instructions for the brand of period underwear you are using.

Tampons

Tampons are a soft, absorbent material that is inserted into the vagina to collect period blood. They have a cotton string which hangs outside the vagina which is used to remove the tampon.

WHERE'S IT GONE?!

Your tampon sits in your vagina. It won't get lost whilst in the vagina because there isn't anywhere for it to go. The vagina leads to the uterus or the womb but the entry (the cervix as we have already learnt) is very narrow and muscular, only allowing fluids to pass through – such as period blood. However, a tampon can travel further up into the vagina, and you may not be able to feel or see the string; this usually happens when someone forgets they have a tampon already in before putting another one in – but there's nothing to worry about, it happens to a lot of folks. You may struggle to reach the tampon, but the vagina is only roughly three to four inches deep, so either remove it yourself or a doctor or even a friend/partner can help you out – remember, relax your body and self to give yourself a better chance of removing it.

WHY DOES INSERTING A TAMPON HURT?

You shouldn't be able to feel a tampon when it's inside you, they are designed to fit into the vagina and to not be felt, so if you can feel it or if it's painful to insert or use, then something may be up. It can take time getting used to using tampons, it can be an artform, so if you're struggling that's ok, you won't be the first! It's ok to feel anxious or stressed or worried when trying tampons at any age, and just know, you don't have to use them if you don't want to! If you do want to give them a try, it's best to try a tampon during your heaviest flow. It's also important to know how to angle your tampon; the vagina doesn't go straight up, so when you insert a tampon, always angle towards your lower back.

Some folks develop Toxic Shock Syndrome, which is caused by a bacterial infection. The risk of Toxic Shock Syndrome is relatively high when using tampons, but you can also develop it through burns, skin wounds or surgical infections. So, why tampons? Well, it isn't totally clear, but due to the fibres of many tampons, bacteria can creep in-between them and then travel into the body when inserted. It can also occur if the tampon has been left in the body for too long. Symptoms include headaches, vomiting, diarrhoea, low blood pressure, redness of eyes, mouth and throat, rashes, a sudden fever and even seizures. But Toxic Shock is very rare, and knowing the symptoms means you can reduce the risk of it acting fast.

Whichever period product you use is totally valid. There is no 'hierarchy of period products'. You don't 'graduate' to tampons. Use whichever feels best to you.

The rainbow of period blood

Period blood can vary in colour, from person to person, from period to period, from the start of your period to the end, but it's totally normal if:

- your period blood isn't red. Period blood can range between a bright pink to red to a brown
- the colour of the blood changes during your period
- the blood is watery or thick (consistency again is unique and can change from one day to the next)
- you see 'lumps' in your blood. Don't worry, these are blood clots and totally normal (though it can be surprising to see them for the first time)
- you see some spots of blood a few days before or a few days after your period.

When to see a professional...

As I keep saying, our bodies and experiences are unique, and our periods are just the same. What one person considers 'normal' may be what someone else considers abnormal in relation to their own experience – but there are some things that can occur which should be raised with a professional if you experience them.* Now, I'm not saying if you experience the following on a

---

* I *really* do not like the word 'normal' for a variety of reasons; however, when talking about our health and bodies, sometimes it's important to know what the 'standard' is and what we should look out for. No one is 'normal' but that's another topic!

regular basis that you are abnormal, but it may be worth booking an appointment with your doctor *just* in case.

- ⊙ A change in the consistency/the flow of your period
- ⊙ Large blood clots that are bigger than a 10p coin
- ⊙ Abnormal heavy bleeding that isn't usual to you. If you're bleeding through 'heavy-flow' or 'night-time' period pads or tampons in a couple of hours, check in with your doctor
- ⊙ Irregular spotting between periods that catch you off guard
- ⊙ Bleeding for more than a week, or bleeding once every week
- ⊙ Not having a period for months
- ⊙ Pain in your abdomen whether you're bleeding or not
- ⊙ Intense mood swings that impact your everyday activities.

Period pain is not just 'period pain'

Yes, periods can hurt, but excruciating pain which leaves you unable to do everyday activities or bed-bound is not normal and should not be just brushed off your shoulder. Endometriosis (or endo) is the second most common gynaecological condition in the UK, impacting up to 10 per cent of folks with a uterus between the ages of 15 and 44. That's 190 million people around the world... yet most folks don't know what it is, or the signs to look out for. Endo is a chronic disease where tissue like that found in the womb grows outside the uterus, causing life-impacting side effects including pain during penetrative sex, urination and bowel movements, bloating, nausea, fatigue, infertility, depression and anxiety. Unfortunately, there is no known cure for endo, though there are ways of controlling the symptoms.

LGBTQ+ folks and periods can be a tricky thing

Periods can make anyone feel uncomfortable in their body and self, but for LGBTQ+ folks, particularly trans people, periods can be a real source of dysphoria. Periods can also directly challenge a trans person's expression and identity. This can make it difficult to:

- see and deal with period blood (which is why some trans folks may choose to use period boxers that are washable)
- insert a tampon or period cup into their vagina (like me! I use period boxers and period pads to avoid this)
- wear a chest binder when their chest is tender
- use a toilet in public which doesn't have a way of disposing period products or purchasing period products.

Some trans folks may choose to use contraception methods which stop their periods altogether.

Period sex is sex

Finally, I want to talk about period sex. Some folks choose to have sex when on their period and that is completely a-ok! Nothing happens during your period which would make sex impossible, but it's completely down to everyone involved if they wish to have sex when a period is involved. The only difference between sex when not on your period and sex on your period is that it will be messier and, well, bloody, but as long as you're comfortable with that and your partner/s is too, then it's down to you whether you have sex on your period or not. Also, it isn't as bloody as you may think – no, it isn't a crime scene or that iconic *Carrie* scene, you may simply have a few red marks or stains on the bed and residue on the condom.

Chapter 4
Beyond Straight and Gay

LGB... easy as 123...

Your sexuality is who you are attracted to, whether that's sexually or romantically. On the Genderbread person illustration (see Chapter 1), it's found in the heart – how cute! Just as with gender, sexuality can also be fluid and change over time, even multiple times over the course of your life. Someone may choose to come out multiple times throughout their life as they learn about new labels and experience new things.

I identified as *bisexual* when I first came out in secondary school (I was outed rather than came out, but more on that later), then a few years later I realized I was *pansexual* because I was attracted to everyone, of all genders. Then in my 20s I came across the label *queer* and thought, 'Hey, this label feels neat, let me try it on for size', and it fitted like a glove – perfection. My journey with sexuality is a common one; as you grow you also may grow out of labels and adopt new ones that fit you better.

There are many ways of being attracted to someone and many different labels folks may use to describe their attraction style and type. Some folks are only romantically attracted to specific folks, some are sexually attracted to everyone, some people aren't too sure who makes their heart flutter and their stomach fill with butterflies, some aren't attracted sexually or romantically to anyone – all are totally valid. Sexuality is not a choice. It can't be influenced or changed; it can't be 'corrected' as there isn't anything wrong with your sexuality.

As with everything that makes us *us*, sexuality exists on... say it with me... a spectrum.

Sexuality can be just as confusing as gender, and like gender, it's ok if you don't have all the answers about your own sexuality or about the world of sexuality. There are many words used to describe sexualities and attractions, with new labels being introduced every day to describe people's identities in a more concise way. Perhaps you get butterflies in your stomach over one type of person, or maybe you blush over different types of people, or maybe you don't get weak knees or sweaty palms for anyone – guess what, that's all ok! There will be others like you out there who feel the same way and even a label that defines your experience which you can use if you want to! Much like gender, sexuality has umbrella terms, broader explanations of attraction, and micro-labels, with more concise definitions that help differentiate one from another.

There are also many acronyms used to encapsulate all these identities, including:

⊙ LGBT (Lesbian, Gay, Bisexual, Transgender)
⊙ LGBT+ (The plus incorporates all the identities which don't fall under 'LGBT', but many feel that stating these four identities but reducing the others to a plus is invalidating or creates a hierarchy of gays.)

- ◉ LGBTQ+ (Lesbian, Gay, Bisexual, Transgender, Queer)
- ◉ LGBTQIA+ (Lesbian, Gay, Bisexual, Transgender, Queer, Intersex, Asexual/Aromantic)
- ◉ LGBTQQIAAP+ (Lesbian, Gay, Bisexual, Transgender, Queer, Questioning, Intersex, Asexual, Aromantic, Pansexual).*

Which acronym is the right one to use? I like to use LGBTQIA+ or LGBTQ+; the reasoning is simply because I like the way that it rolls off the tongue and I can say it quickly, but each person has their own preference and it's ok to use any of these acronyms. You'll probably not see many people using LGBTQQIAAP+ because it's quite a mouthful, but it's good to see identities getting the representation they deserve.

What is 'alphabet soup'?

Alphabet soup is a phrase you may have heard of to refer to the entire LGBTQIA+ community without using the acronym. It highlights how many amazing identities there are out there, and I personally really love the term, we are all in this big warm soup together, trying to figure it all out. Swimming around helplessly. And we taste fantastic!

---

* You may be asking, 'Dee, why are there a mixture of gender identities and sexualities in these acronyms? And why have you put this in the Sexuality chapter?' Well even though sexuality and gender are different parts of our identities, the fight for our rights as a community is one that we all share. Regardless of your sexuality or gender identity, if you identify as anything other than straight or cisgender, you may be targeted because of your identity. You may be a victim of a hate crime, or violence, or have your rights either taken from you, or not there to begin with – so as a community, we share this pain, and therefore, we must come together as a community – hence the acronyms!

The gay animal planet

I knew I wanted to dedicate a small section of this chapter to the queer beauty of nature, so here we go. Yes, queerness is 100 per cent totally natural and is found in nature in many different creatures and plants. Same-sex behaviour has been found in roughly 1500 species, including penguins, lions, bottlenose dolphins, orcas, monkeys and lizards. Did you know the oldest animal in the world is queer! Jonathan, a 190-year-old tortoise in St Helena, has a boyfriend and they have been together for over three decades. Goals AF. Lions too are known to couple up with their own gender. That's right, the king of the jungle is more of a queen. And if you think we have many labels, the multi-sexed fungi (the Schizophyllum commune) has more than 23,000 sexual identities.

Heterosexual

Some folks are heterosexual, or 'straight'. This means they are attracted to folks of a different gender to them (I say different as opposite implies there are only two genders, and we know that isn't the case). A trans woman who is dating a man may identify as straight, a cis man dating a cis woman may use the label heterosexual, a trans man may date a trans woman and identify as straight – all are valid. If someone says they use a certain label, and identify as a specific identity, they are valid in doing so – regardless of what anyone else says.

We've already explored the acronym LGBTQIA+ but now let's deep dive into the various labels and identities that fall within the acronym. As there are a fair few to go through, we will be discussing them in alphabet order, not the acronym order.

Before that though, remember we spoke about umbrella terms

and micro-labels? Well, the identities we are going to explore will consist of umbrella terms and micro-labels which sit under their respective umbrellas. We may not go through every single micro-label, as new ones are added constantly, but we will go through as many as possible.

Ace umbrella

Aromantic

Describes folks who have little to no romantic attraction to others, though they may experience sexual attraction.

Asexual

An asexual person is someone who rarely or never experiences sexual attraction. They may have romantic attractions and relationships but are generally not interested in sex. Asexual individuals are not choosing abstinence, they simply do not want to have sex with others or aren't generally interested in it. Asexual, sometimes abbreviated to Ace, folks can be of any gender identity or romantic attraction, though in the 2022 Asexual Census, it was found that many asexual individuals are trans and nonbinary – neat! Asexual individuals face erasure and discrimination in a higher capacity than other members of the LGBTQIA+ community, mostly due to the misconception that asexuality isn't real. The first ever Ace Report, created by Stonewall and Activist Yasmin Benoit, revealed that Ace people are less likely to be open about their orientation to friends and family – with analysis of government data showing that only one in four (26.1%) asexual people are open about their sexuality with friends.*

---

*   www.stonewall.org.uk/resources/ace-report

Fluid sexualities (abro lesbian, aceflux, autoflexible, biflux, greymasfluid, petosexual, oscillsexual)

These are all sexualities which are fluid in some way. For example, aceflux is a sexual orientation on the asexual spectrum. It is defined as someone whose sexual orientation fluctuates but generally stays on the asexual spectrum.

G – greysexual, grey-Ace, grey asexual

This term falls under the asexual umbrella used by those who identify as asexual but don't feel as if they totally fit into that label. Greysexual, or graysexual, is also an umbrella term itself, including sex-repulsed, sex-positive and sex-neutral individuals.

- ⊙ Sex-repulsed: Folks who are completely disinterested and repulsed by sex.
- ⊙ Sex-neutral: Folks who aren't disinterested in sex but don't necessarily seek it out. They may have sex if they want to but aren't actively looking for pleasure.
- ⊙ Sex-positive: Folks who aren't sexually attracted to individuals but still may have sex for pleasure.

Other Ace identities:

- ⊙ Demisexual
- ⊙ Demiromantic
- ⊙ Greysexual
- ⊙ Greyromantic
- ⊙ Libidoist asexual
- ⊙ Lithromantic
- ⊙ Quoiromantic
- ⊙ Cupioromantic
- ⊙ Sex-averse
- ⊙ Sex-favourable
- ⊙ Sex-indifferent.

How can we best support our Ace siblings? Acknowledging and

educating others on the fact that not everyone wants to have sex is a start. Challenging anti-Ace comments and discrimination, standing up for Ace folks, including Ace folks in your conversations around sexuality and accepting Ace folks for who they are are all things everyone should be doing.

Multisexual umbrella

Multisexual is an umbrella term for folks who experience attraction to multiple genders. Bisexual, pansexual, polysexual and omnisexual fall under this umbrella.

Bisexual, bicurious

Though there is a misconception that bisexuality means attraction to men and women (or two genders), the term is best defined as an attraction to two or more genders. This includes trans and nonbinary individuals. Bicurious is defined as someone who is curious about people of different genders but isn't totally sure yet how they would label themselves.

Bisexual individuals face biphobia and discrimination from those who do not believe bisexuality is a real thing, or that bisexual people are simply sex-crazed fiends. Bi folks are three times less likely than gay men and lesbians to come out to their family or friends for these very reasons.*

Omnisexual

Omnisexual describes folks who are attracted to people of all genders, but with a preference for certain genders.

---

* www.stonewall.org.uk/about-us/news/new-research-bi-people-less-likely-be-out

Pansexual, polysexual

No, pansexuals aren't attracted to frying pans. Pansexual individuals are attracted to people of all genders with zero preference for gender. This isn't to say that they are attracted to everyone, but rather can be attracted to anyone.

Polysexual individuals are attracted to multiple genders but not all genders. This is like bisexual individuals. Some polysexual folks may also use bi to describe their attraction, whilst others believe bisexuality doesn't cover the entirety of their attraction.

Other multisexual identities

- ◎ Agentosexual
- ◎ Heteroflexible
- ◎ Homoflexible
- ◎ Ambisexual.

Lesbian

A lesbian is a woman who is attracted to other women or non-men who love non-men. Originally, and still to this day, some folks use the acronym WLW (women loving women); however, this acronym can be exclusive to gender-diverse+ individuals who are lesbians. As we've already learnt, trans women can be lesbians, nonbinary folks and gender-diverse+ folks can be lesbians. But why is 'L' at the start of the acronym? Well, there actually is a reason why the L is at the beginning and it's a very important one. L is at the start of the acronym to honour the lesbians who stood by gay men during the HIV/AIDS epidemic, as a message of solidarity and of hope for continued solidarity in the future.

Queer, questioning

Queer is another umbrella term, like gay, which can be used by anyone within the LGBTQIA+ community. Queer is both an umbrella term and an identity label by itself.

Queer has a long history of being a slur used against LGBTQIA+ members, which is why you might find older generations of LGBTQIA+ folks not wishing to be referred to as queer, which is totally valid.* If someone says they don't want to be referred to as a label, they must be respected in that decision. Even if how they identify sounds really like how you do and you use the term queer, they get to decide which label suits them. It's also good to use the term LGBTQIA+ when referring to the wider community because, as I said, not everyone will feel comfortable being referred to as queer. However, younger generations of queer folks have reclaimed the term, using it not only to refer to the entire community, but themselves, their culture, their style and just about anything and everything about themselves! I use queer to describe my sexual attraction, my gender, my expression, my taste in literature, movies, tattoos, hobbies, my tribe and my relationship. I also like how ambiguous queer can be. Is it describing someone's sexuality, gender, expression? Who knows! It's a mystery. I love it!

---

* It was at university when I first realized that some older LGBTQIA+ people don't like using the term 'queer'. One of my lecturers posed the question to me of 'why do you use queer to encapsulate the whole community?' and I was taken aback. After a whole class conversation, he told us that, as a gay man, using the term queer for him brings up a lot of painful memories of being bullied or hate-crimed, so he prefers to use 'gay' or LGBTQIA+ for the community. It's fascinating how different generations have different feelings towards terms and language that we refer to ourselves with.

Questioning is exactly what it says, it's when someone is questioning their sexuality and doesn't want to jump into a specific label or community yet. Questioning folks are just as valid as someone who has a label.

Sapphic

'She was a Sapphic' – TikTok has taken over my brain, please tell me you remember that sound! Sapphic is an umbrella term used by anyone who is attracted to women other than cis men and originates from the lesbian poet Sappho. This can include women, nonbinary folks and gender-diverse+ folks who are attracted to women. This term can be used by those who identify as multisexual too, it doesn't exclude attraction to men, it's more about the identity of the person who is attracted to women.

Other identities

- Monosexual
- Pomosexual
- Skoliosexual
- Spectrosexual
- Androsexual
- Gynesexual.

Oof, that's a lot of labels!

Also, this list may be dated by the time you read it as we are adding labels and identities every single day!

Sexual attraction vs romantic attraction

Some folks are only sexually attracted to people, some folks are only romantically attracted to folks, some folks are sexually and romantically attracted to folks, and some have zero attraction. You may also have a different type of sexual attraction to romantic attraction.

Romantic attraction

Romantic attraction is when someone desires a loving connection with someone and wishes to form a long-lasting bond. Someone who experiences romantic attractions only will want to spend time with another person, take them on dates, be their partner, but not necessarily want to have sex with them.

Under the romantic attraction umbrella, you have:

⊙ Abroromantic – which describes someone whose romantic attraction is fluid and/or changing over time.

⊙ Aromantic – someone who doesn't experience romantic attraction at all, or at a very low rate.

⊙ Androromantic – someone who is romantically attracted to men, males and masculinity (including gender-diverse+ individuals who are masc-presenting).

⊙ Biromantic – those who are romantically attracted to two or more genders.

⊙ Demiromantic – which describes someone who doesn't experience romantic attraction until they form a deep emotional connection with someone.

⊙ Gyneromantic – someone who is romantically attracted to women, females and femininity (including gender-diverse+ folks who are femme-presenting).

⊙ Panromantic – someone who is romantically attracted to people of all genders.

- Polyromantic – someone who is romantically attracted to many people but not all genders.

Label-less? Ok!

I am someone who has struggled with labels throughout my time exploring my gender identity and sexuality, and for a while I went label-less. Some folks don't want to put themselves into a box, to iden-tify their attraction to other people, or simply they haven't found a term that truly reflects how they feel yet, so they decide to not use a label at all. And many folks are de-ciding to go label-less. For me, and many others, labels can feel restrictive or unchangeable; once you commit to a label it can feel as if you must use that one label forever, particularly if you tell other people. But that's not the case at all. You can change your label at any time, as many times as you want or need to because, as with everything else in our lives, things change!

I've changed labels to describe my sexuality many times – from bisexual, to pansexual, to label-less, to queer. I came out as bisexual as a teen; well, I didn't come out – I was outed. I had told a close friend that I was bisexual, as teens do, I wanted to share that information with a bestie, and as she was gay, I thought my secret was safe. Unfortunately, she was bullied heavily for being gay, being a masc-butch girl, people assumed she was gay even if she hadn't told them. On one occasion the bullying got so bad I had to speak up, but by speaking up and telling the other pupils to cut it out, they hit me with 'what, are you gay too?' and I guess I was so full of adrenaline I said 'no, I'm bi'. This isn't the same as other individuals who are outed by other people, I know that, but I do think the situation I was put in, the response the pupils gave when I decided to speak up, forced me into a situation I couldn't escape from. I wasn't ready to come out but, at that moment, I couldn't stop it. I then was also bullied for being 'another queer'.

I hadn't really put much thought into my sexuality, but I did know I found people of different genders attractive, and I knew I wasn't straight or gay... so I guessed I must be bisexual. There weren't any other labels that I knew of, so I just assumed I was bi and that was that. After a few years, I discovered the term pansexual and, suddenly, that felt like it fitted me way more than bi ever did. So, I dropped bi and took pansexual for a try. However, it was then that I learnt how much erasure multisexual folks experience. Someone I was close to at the time told me one day that I couldn't be pansexual because I 'hadn't been with a girl' and that pansexuality wasn't real anyway, that it was just another word for bi. At the time I didn't know very much about erasure and panphobia, so I didn't know that he was just being an idiot, so I dropped pansexual and went back to bi. Note to any pansexual folks out there: you are valid, and no, you're not 'just bi'. Also, your sexual history has *zero* to do with your sexuality, ok? But again, bisexual didn't feel right – so I went label-less.

Then the pandemic hit and suddenly I was given all this spare time to explore my identity and research into what my feelings towards others meant (and by research, I mean spend hours on TikTok watching other people's coming-out stories, thirst-traps, queer history videos). It was then that I discovered queer, and the pieces fell into place. It's the label I've used for the past 3+ years and I don't think I will ever drop it. As I said, queer feels like home, it feels warm, it feels cosy, it describes every part of me. At the time, each of those labels felt like they described how I felt perfectly, but over time, they started to feel restrictive. I was just as valid using any of those previous labels as I am now using queer and will be if I change my labels in the future. Sometimes it takes trial and error, some experimenting to figure out what labels suit you and feel just right, and that's something you may go through multiple times in your life.*

If labelling yourself just isn't for you, that's a-ok! There is certainly freedom in being label-less and simply existing as you. Don't get me wrong, some folks love labels and love being able to identify and describe their feelings. Since discovering queer I certainly feel at home in myself and I adore the label, it feels like home. Putting a name to how you feel also means you can find your community, folks who have similar attraction types and styles. You find your own tribe. And this can be crucial for many folks exploring their sexuality, people who are newly out, finding others who feel the same as you, people you can look up, folks who can give you advice. Label or no-label, you are valid.

You are always 'queer enough'!

You are queer enough. You are always enough.

But let's get into why you may not feel that way. Self-acceptance is one of the hardest things LGBTQIA+ folks go through when questioning and figuring out their identity. And at the root of this

---

* Whilst writing this book I've gone through a few different labels myself!

inability to truly accept who we are inside and out is internalized homophobia. This is where an individual may not feel comfortable in their identity and accept who they are.

Internalized homophobia can hit you from several angles. Internalized homophobia can happen because society pushes the narrative that being straight and cisgender is the 'norm' and anything outside of those two identities are 'abnormal', so those who don't fit neatly into those two boxes feel ashamed and confused. Internalized homophobia can also come from a lack of representation which can make people forget that LGBTQIA+ people are all around us, or bad representation which can make people not want to be associated with LGBTQIA+ people or the community, or poor representation which can make someone believe they need to fit into stereotypes to be considered 'real' and valid. It can also come from family attitudes, culture, faith, friends, partners, media, literature – basically most places!

In short, internalized homophobia makes you believe that being LGBTQIA+ is wrong, or something to be ashamed of, something to keep a secret, something to pray away. But as we have learnt, you are completely valid in your identity. There is no right or wrong when it comes to sexuality, and there shouldn't be any shame in who you want to be romantic with or sexual with (as long as they are of legal age and consent). You can't change who you are, and you can't change who you are attracted to.

By the way, you can have internalized biphobia, panphobia, transphobia and so on!

You may hear LGBTQIA+ folks say 'I don't feel queer enough', or 'I don't feel trans enough', or maybe even you've said or felt this way before. This is something I have battled with ever since I came out as bi, then pan, then queer, then nonbinary and trans, and it's something I felt all the way up till I was in my mid-20s, at the exact time I began writing this book, in fact. For many years I feared not looking 'queer enough', or that I wasn't queer enough because I hadn't ever been intimate with someone who wasn't a man (which has now changed), and it didn't help that someone I trusted also affirmed that misconception.

Accepting who we are is a huge step in our journeys, whether that's in our sexuality or gender journey. Some folks accept who they are quicker than others, and that may be because they have a more supportive network of LGBTQIA+ friendly individuals, or maybe they were raised by other LGBTQIA+ people. Either way, your journey to self-acceptance is your own. If you are struggling with truly accepting the individual you are, find your community, trusted allies or other LGBTQIA+ folks you can talk to, find media that reflects your experience (when I watched *Feel Good* with Mae Martin for the first time, I finally understood what nonbinaryness meant to me, it was like the puzzle pieces just fell into place and I am forever grateful to that series for that) and be kind to yourself. You'll get there.

The closet is cosy for some, but others want to come out!

Being in the 'closet' or 'being closeted' is when you haven't come out yet or told anyone how you identify or have only told specific people. Unfortunately, we live in a society where we are assumed to be cisgender and heterosexual until we say we aren't, which is why LGBTQIA+ folks come out.

Whether you come out or not, you're just as valid in your identity and you should never feel as if you *must* come out to be valid.

It is totally, 100 per cent your choice whether you tell someone or anyone about your identity. Some folks may never want to come out, perhaps they aren't able to or simply don't care what other people think about their identity and want to keep it private. Why do straight people get away with not having to shout to the world that they are straight, huh? Why do queer people have to tell others how they identify? That's how some LGBTQIA+ folks feel and it's why they may not openly tell people their label, rather they just go about their life.

Some folks may decide to anonymously come out online, creating a private social media page for them to explore their identity without people knowing who they are or only their close friends having access. This allows for you to find your community and to trial how coming out feels for you, whether it's something you want to do publicly or something you prefer to keep private. When I first started to question my gender identity as a teen, wayyy before I knew nonbinary existed, I would use online platforms to explore and experiment with my gender. I created a private Instagram page where I could be me away from the eyes of people who knew me, and although I deleted the page quickly out of anxiety and fear of being caught, that experience has stuck with me and, now I'm an out enby, I'm proud of baby me for taking that step.

Some folks may only tell a select few people who they feel safe telling – this can be called 'situational coming out', which is where someone may come out to specific people or be out in a specific environment or situation. But why would someone only come out in certain spaces? Well, not every space is safe for queer folks to be visible, perhaps you're in a new environment and fearful of being accepted, so you decide to not come out in that space. Or say you haven't told your family yet, so when you're at a family gathering, you don't share that part of you with them. Some folks may not have the privilege of being able to be public about their identity, and if you think coming out may be dangerous to you, or put you in a tricky situation, consider whether you want or need to come out. Though coming out is seen as this huge moment for many LGBTQIA+ people, a moment to celebrate, it isn't possible or safe for everyone to do this and that should always be respected. Our safety as individuals should always be a priority, and sadly that may mean not publicly sharing your identity at this time.

There are many reasons why someone may only come out to certain people or be out in certain spaces. If someone has recently figured out their sexuality, they may want to tell a few close friends but may not be ready to tell the world yet or it isn't safe to tell anyone else yet. Telling close friends who you trust is a great way to feel affirmed in your identity and to see how coming out feels to you. It's important that if someone is only out to you or out in specific places that you don't out them outside of those who know and that space. If you don't want to tell your friends but need advice, find a trusted adult to speak to, or a doctor. If it's possible, you may be able to find a community space or group of other queer folks you can hang out with who understand what you're going through.

Coming out isn't a one-time thing. Some folks come out multiple times in their life, some come out multiple times in a year. Figuring out who we are and what labels to describe our feelings isn't easy, and sometimes we use a label that doesn't fit us for a long time. Coming out more than once doesn't invalidate who you were and who you are after coming out again. It doesn't mean how you identified before was 'wrong' or that it was a 'phase'.

Also, most of us will come out various times a day to different people. I have come out so many times in my life, either as a new identity, using a new label, or just to new people. In the last week I have come out to my doctor, my new therapist, my mortgage adviser, multiple people at work, online and the list continues. If you're trans or gender-diverse+, you also have to come out in terms of your gender on the daily too. Double coming out. We come out soooo many times in life, and most of the time in a very casual way. Coming out isn't always a big moment, sometimes it's simply using 'partner' when talking about your relationship.

You get to decide whether you come out and in what capacity you come out in.

Some folks are the come-outer, and others are the ones we come out to

How do you react if someone comes out to you? It's not something we are ever taught, rather it's something we either awkwardly learn how to do ourselves or we google once someone has come out to us and we had no idea what to say or do. It can be difficult to know what to say and do when someone comes out to you, especially if you're not LGBTQIA+ yourself.

For some, coming out is huge, and those individuals are usually the most anxious about coming out to you (or anyone), so being supportive and giving them a hug can be a great place to start. For others who come out casually, mid-conversation or via text, a more casual 'thanks for telling me' works. Regardless of how the person comes out to you, saying 'thank you for telling me' is important because it shows the other person that you know how big of a deal it was to share that with you and how grateful you are that they chose you to tell. When someone comes out, they want to be accepted and reassured, so a thank you goes a long way.

Not everyone will know what a label or sexuality or gender identity means, but it's important to not force the individual who has come out into the 'teacher role'. If possible, wait until you're alone and do your own research into the label and identity, and if you still have questions after, then you can ask the person. This isn't to say you can't or shouldn't ask questions when they first come out to you, but it's best to not bombard them with what, how, why etc. You can ask things like 'how can I refer to you?' or 'what pronouns or name should I use?' or 'what words can I use to describe who you date?' or 'is there anything I can do to help or support you?' – those questions are ok as they show you actively want to be an ally and support the individual.

Avoid saying things like:

- ⊙ I always knew!
- ⊙ We could tell!
- ⊙ But you don't look xyz!
- ⊙ I don't need to know about your sex life!
- ⊙ Keep it to yourself!

Lady Gaga, you can keep 'Born this way'

I'm going to say it, I'm a hater. I really dislike how this catchy slogan became an all-encompassing statement for the queer community because, frankly, it isn't my experience, and it isn't everyone's truth. I do appreciate what Gaga's lyrics did for the community, how it was claimed by the queer community and used to fight for our rights and political change, heck it was integral for legalizing marriage equality in the UK. But I do think it lacks nuance and I knew I had to get this off my chest in this chapter. The gist of the lyric is that LGBTQIA+ folks deserve their rights and freedoms because their queerness is innate and natural – which it totally is. Queerness is all around us (as we touched on before in animals!). And the phrase does tackle the misconception that queerness is a choice, and in that respect, I enjoy the phrase. However, the phrase seems to leave out the prospect of change, of our sexuality and gender being fluid, and for someone who has come out various times, the phrase just doesn't fit me. It also ignores the fact that our gender and sexuality can evolve over time, and how that is just as valid as someone who has always known their sexuality or gender.

Does that mean I am boycotting the phrase and petitioning for it to be removed from our queer vocab? Of course not! But I do want allies and other LGBTQIA+ folks to understand why some queer people dislike the phrase, or don't feel included in it. Whether you like and use the phrase or not, that's down to you. Lady Gaga, your song is a bop, but I may sit 'Born this way' out.

Discrimination and knowing your rights as an LGBTQIA+ person

Let's get real. LGBTQIA+ people are facing higher levels of discrimination each year. As new laws are brought in that further restrict or completely erase LGBTQIA+ people's rights all around the globe, our community is facing a new wave of hate, particularly trans and gender-diverse+ individuals. In the US, 583 anti-trans bills were brought to attention in 2023, and of those 583, 85 passed and, at the time of writing, 373 were active. As of October 2023, conversion therapy is still not banned in the UK, nonbinary is not legally recognized, trans kids can be outed to their possible anti-trans households by teachers, and that's just the tip of the iceberg. As you may have noticed, most of the laws or bills I have mentioned are relating to trans folks, and that's because that is the community currently under most attack. This is why trans protests and prides have been so crucial within the last few years, to come together to vocalize our pain and to demand our rights, to celebrate our transness, and to find community in dark times. Organizations, campaigns and charities that raise awareness about the difficulties trans individuals and the wider queer community are facing and supporting them through services such as helplines, therapy, housing etc are vital.

Trans Kids Deserve to Grow Up*

In 2023, I started my campaign *Trans Kids Deserve to Grow Up* in response to the direct attack towards our trans youth by the government. It was through this campaign I really found my voice within activism, as a trans individual, and found others who were just as vocal, both within and outside the trans community.

Why am I mentioning my campaign in this chapter? Well, for three reasons. One, because I am incredibly proud of the campaign, and the awareness and support it has provided for trans youth, their families and teachers. Two, because I found my voice through founding this campaign. I realized how important my voice as a trans individual is, how impactful my experience is, how my contacts and resources can help other individuals, and how vital it is to be vocal not only for my community but others who are

---

* See @transkidsdeservetogrowup or search for #transkidsdeservetogrowup.

also facing discrimination and hate. And, finally, three, because I want to remind you that you too can be part of a movement or even start your own. If you're passionate about something, or want to see something change in the world, if you have the capacity to do so, be vocal. For many folks, getting into activism can be intimidating, or it may feel as if you don't have a voice within that space – but you do, and you can if you want to. My campaign started one night in my bedroom after reading the leaked Trans Student Guidance; with just a concept and a hashtag, it became a national solidarity campaign. If you want to fight for something, go for it!

But why would someone not support you?

This is a question I've asked myself many times, and I think many queer people do too. Why would someone not want to support you in being your true self? That just seems like something everyone would want, right? There are many reasons why acceptance is not always the case, and I want to go through them because knowing why can sometimes help LGBTQIA+ people navigate the world and stay safe.

In some places, being LGBTQIA+ is illegal and considered a crime. As we have already explored, discrimination towards LGBTQIA+ people is on the rise, and due to this, laws and bills are being implemented globally. Though of course, within those countries and states, there are individuals who will support you, but many may fear accepting your identity because of the legal implications, or the social beliefs which have helped those laws come into place. Religion also plays a huge role in this, with many anti-LGBTQIA+ people claiming that their faith doesn't support queer people, meaning they can't either. These institutional reasons can be hard to combat and navigate, particularly for queer people born into them. Sometimes that's all people have known, that LGBTQIA+ identities are 'legally or morally wrong', and changing that perception can be a difficult and long process. But regardless of whether you live in a country or state that has these laws, or whichever faith you belong to, you will still come across people who will accept and support you.

But mostly, people who struggle to accept LGBTQIA+ identities simply don't understand them because they aren't part of that community, and lack of understanding leads to fear and hate, which isn't helped when the media pushes certain stereotypes of LGBTQIA+ individuals which further support this confusion and fear. Most of the hate I receive is from individuals who try to push 'facts' – 'there are only two genders', 'you're either straight or gay', 'nonbinary isn't real' – which they have been fed since they were kids, and when someone's understanding is challenged, when they are presented with new ideas, this can intimidate them and can result in bullying, harassment, discrimination and hate. Unfortunately, many of these individuals simply don't want to learn, which is why I don't waste my energy trying to 'prove' myself because it's pointless. However, this isn't always the case and I've had really amazing conversations with people who actively listened to what I had to say and accepted that their experience wasn't the only one out there. As a queer person, it's important to know that you sadly can't change everyone's mind and it's not your job to do so.

And sometimes, those who hurt LGBTQIA+ people may also be questioning their identity. Now I really dislike the 'bully is gay-in-denial' rhetoric and trope most often seen in teen movies, but in some cases, that is people's truth. Some folks who strug-gle with accepting themselves may take it out on those who do accept themselves, or have supportive families, or aren't battling the institutional beliefs we just spoke about.

In-fighting

And sadly, a lot of discrimination and hate comes from within our own community. As a trans and nonbinary individual, I have been discriminated against by trans people who don't think I'm trans enough, or who don't believe nonbinary is a 'real thing'. I've also been discriminated against by nonbinary individuals who, again, don't think I'm androgynous enough to be nonbinary. And I've re-ceived the most hate from other members of the LGBTQ+ commu-nity for being gender-diverse+. It's something that I think hurts more than being discriminated against by cisgender or straight people, because these are members of our community who should see that we are one and the same, yet sadly, they don't. And I'm not saying I would rather be discriminated by cis or straight peo-ple, I would love to be accepted by all, but it hurts on another level when it's other queer people.*

---

* At the time of writing this I have just entered my first T4T relationship (more on that shortly) and have shared my experience of giving head to a vulva owner for the first time. Sadly, though the post was about my personal experience and was a celebratory moment, many people from my own com-munity said my experience wasn't valid or that I was taking up space that other members deserved. All LGBTQIA+ people should be allowed to celebrate their joyful moments without others jumping on it to destroy it. It really upset me but sadly that's what is happening in our community at the moment. We need to come together guys!

Gatekeeping

Gatekeeping is *not* girlbossing.

When you're exploring your identity, or what labels to use, you may meet people who try to tell you what and how you should and shouldn't identify. This is called gatekeeping, and you've probably heard this term being thrown around on TikTok. An example of gatekeeping I've experienced is people telling me that I can't be nonbinary because I occasionally wear skirts or makeup or don't experience dysphoria about my chest 24/7. This is completely inaccurate – as we have learnt, transness and queerness is whatever we want it to be and that's why gatekeeping is harmful, particularly for young and newly out LGBTQIA+ individuals. However one chooses to identify or label themselves to express themselves is valid and shouldn't be questioned. And yes, sometimes gatekeeping can come from someone who truly wants to help and be supportive, but even in these situations, it's important to acknowledge that your experience is unique to you and you don't have to listen or take someone's 'advice' if you don't want to!

A isn't for Ally – but we appreciate you!

No, the A in LGBTQIA+ isn't for Ally; however, it is important we talk about our allies here.

An ally is someone who supports the people around them usually to reach a common goal; for an LGBTQIA+ ally, this means supporting and fighting for people's right to love who they want to love and be who they want to be. Being an ally isn't always about the big things; in reality, the small everyday allyship goes a long way to make queer folks feel accepted, respected and cared for.

Easy ways to be an A-star ally:

⊙ Stand up for LGBTQIA+ rights; this may look like attending protests, signing petitions, sharing information, voting etc.

⊙ Be vocal, again attending protests, being public about your support for LGBTQIA+ rights and people.

⊙ Be open minded; just because you may not understand something, or feel a certain way about your identity, doesn't mean that how others feel is invalid or 'wrong'. You just have a different experience to them, and understanding that, and keeping an open mind, is key.

⊙ Call out discrimination and harassment when you see it, holding people accountable.

⊙ Educate others on how to be an LGBTQIA+ ally. It is *not* the role of LGBTQIA+ individuals to educate everyone, and though some of us enjoy it (aka me), it still gets tiring. You can watch a YouTube video, or follow a queer Tik-Toker, or read a book like this one, or watch a documentary, or google a question you have, and once you know these things, you can pay it forward by sharing your new knowledge with other allies.

⊙ Listen to and check in on LGBTQIA+ people, uplifting their voices and stories.

⊙ Use people's chosen name, pronouns, labels and language.

⊙ Use inclusive language.

⊙ Provide a safe space for LGBTQIA+ people in your workplace, school or home.

Allyship for LGBTQIA+ people is a 24/7, every day of the week act, but the last several years have been extremely difficult for

LGBTQIA+ people around the globe. LGBTQIA+ mental health is at an all-time low. The Trevor Project found that, in 2023, 41 per cent of LGBTQIA+ young people have seriously considered ending their life, with 56 per cent being unable to access mental health support and care.* However, acts of allyship are proven to improve LGBTQIA+ folks' quality of life. The Trevor Project found that trans and nonbinary young people who have their pronouns respected by everyone in their life reported lower rates of considering suicide. Using someone's correct pronoun and name is lifesaving. So, although it may seem like a small thing to someone who has never changed their pronouns or name before, it can make a world of difference to a trans individual, and it really isn't difficult to do!

---

* www.thetrevorproject.org/survey-2023

Chapter 5
Beyond Trousers and Skirts

Expression is how we present ourselves to the world: it's in the clothes we wear, the trends we follow, the hair style, cut and colour we sport and how we navigate society. On the Genderbread person (see Chapter 1), this is found on the outside of the person as this is what people can see.

For all people, cisgender, transgender, nonbinary, queer or heterosexual, expression can be a very important part of their identity as it informs how others perceive and read them (whether someone wants them to or not). It can also be very important for showing other factors of our identity, such as our ethnicity or faith. For example, someone who is religious may wear a cross around their neck, or a hijab; someone who is queer may wear a flag badge on their jacket, or a variety of rings (I wear 12 in total, all at once). Now, you may be thinking that 'rings' don't scream sexuality or queer, but a cross and hijab clearly express religion – well that's one of the beauties of expression, communities can make their own symbols and ways of sharing their identity through clothing and accessories. Historically, different groups of people claim different items of clothing and accessories as a way of expressing themselves to others and new symbols are created every day.

Fun history of lesbians and the Birkenstock

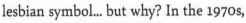

Yes, you heard me right – lesbians have a history with Birkenstock sandals, and if you saw Greta Gerwig's *Barbie* movie, you may have seen the subtle nod to this iconic lesbian symbol... but why? In the 1970s, lesbians chose to appear as 'unfashionable' or 'undesirable' as possible to protest society's beauty standards, and in this protest the Birkenstock became the go-to ugly shoe. This sandal became a political statement against the patriarchy and expectations of women overnight. Birkenstocks become a signal that the individual wearing them was a lesbian and the stereotype was born. In 1992, a *New York Times* piece described how some people view lesbians as women who 'wear only jeans and Birkenstocks'.* And today, lesbians may choose to wear Birkenstocks as a throwback to this movement... or simply because other lesbians wear them!**

Right now, the most common signal of queerness is the carabiner, though many non-queer folks have begun adopting the statement fashion piece, confusing us little gays.

---

* www.nytimes.com/1992/03/31/news/patterns-358192.html
** The patriarchy is a system of society or government in which men hold the power and women are excluded from it.

Gender is one big performance!

You may have heard of the phrase *'gender is a performance'* by the iconic gender theorist Judith Butler. From an early age we are shown symbols that relate to our assigned sex at birth: clothing that we should wear and ways we should behave and play which are different from other children who are assigned the opposite sex at birth. I was taught that 'being a girl', which is what I was assigned as at birth, meant liking Disney princesses, the colour pink, playing with babydolls and Barbies, being polite, feminine and caring – which is why my mother was so unsure when I asked for Power Rangers for Christmas, or wore my hiking boots under my princess dresses, or asked to take up boxing.

Interestingly, in the 20th century, pink was assigned to boys as it was deemed 'ardent', active and aggressive, while blue was assigned to girls as it is a more passive colour. Then, bizarrely, this switched, becoming blue for boys and pink for girls. I have recently become super into the colour pink, reclaiming it as a nonbinary individual who was raised as a girl – so I'm writing this with a silly pink bow in my hair, and that feels like a huge step on my gender journey.***

We are given signs growing up and told how to 'perform' the

*** I'm here to tell you again that not every trans person will refer to their childhood in the same way I do. I use phrases like 'I was raised as a girl' or 'I was viewed as a girl' because my connection to girlhood, and the impact it had on me, both internally and externally within society, has played a huge part in who I am. I am very comfortable talking about my experiences as a girl growing up, but I know many other trans folks avoid these phrases and prefer to use terms that affirm their current identity – both are totally valid! Always ask someone how they wish to refer to their past self (if they even want to) or listen to how they talk about their past self and use that language too.

gender and sex that are assigned at birth, but you get to choose how you express your gender and whether your gender is the same as the one you were assigned at birth. You get to choose how you express yourself to the world, and whether you choose to express your gender through your outward appearance or not. Those who do wish to express their gender in the way that society expects them to are considered 'gender conforming'. Those who express themselves outside of the norms that are attached to their assigned gender at birth are considered 'gender nonconforming'.

Clothing, hairstyles and behaviours have no gender

Though certain clothing, styles and behaviours are socially linked to different genders or sexualities, this doesn't mean these types of expressions are only for specific individuals.

You can define what different expressions mean to you and what they represent; one person's masc outfit may be someone else's fem outfit, and that's ok! Take me, for example, I may wear a dress or skirt sometimes but that doesn't mean I'm now a girl just because skirts are traditionally seen to be for girls and women only, but it also doesn't mean that I see myself as more 'fem' in the skirt. I'm wearing the skirt for me and because I want to, it doesn't feel gendered because it's just cloth. However, an AMAB individual may wear skirts to help them feel more fem and express themselves as more feminine – both of our experiences are valid. If we are really getting into the nitty gritty here, skirts have been worn by all gender identities for centuries – men in the 14th century wore skirts and tights daily. It's completely ok to experiment with your expression, to be fluid with how you present yourself to the world and to go against the 'norms' of what is traditionally associated with your gender. Like gender and sexuality, expression is a spectrum, and how you define your expression and clothing may differ from how someone else describes the same expression – and that's ok. It's also completely ok to not have a fixed expression, to play around with how you present yourself to the world.

For queer and trans people, expression can be either a real source of euphoria or dysphoria.

Euphoria

Euphoria is a powerful feeling of happiness as a result of moving closer to your gender identity.

This can be achieved by:

- ◉ Socially transitioning
    - Transitioning publicly through name and pronoun changes and using your expression to represent your gender identity.
    - I have socially transitioned by using different pronouns from the ones assigned to me at birth and by going by 'Dee' rather than my birth name.
- ◉ Legally transitioning
    - Changing your sex, name and/or pronouns on legal documents.
    - In 2022 I changed my name by deed poll (a legal document that proves your name change) to 'Dee Lou'.
    - Note: At the time of writing this book it is not possible to self-identify as nonbinary within the UK and the

gender-neutral title of 'Mx', pronounced 'mix', which I use, is not universally accepted, or found on all documentation.

⊙ Medically transitioning
   – The act of undergoing sex-affirming surgeries or taking hormones to move closer to one's desired sex/gender.
⊙ Expression
   – Some people will find euphoria in changing their expression and style to match their identity; this can also include binding, tucking or packing.

Binding

Binding is the method of compressing the breast tissue to appear as flat as possible, to achieve a more androgynous or masculine look, either using binding tape or a fabric binder.

ARE BINDERS DANGEROUS?

Most binders are safe, but they do come with risks, especially when not worn correctly or for too long. You shouldn't wear a binder for more than six to eight hours per day, or sleep in them, and if you do exercise or have sex in them, it's important you consider whether the activity will be intense or not (more on this soon!). You should be able to fit two fingers between your binder and your skin and be able to move around in it without being winded and breathing normally.

But why shouldn't you wear a binder for long periods? Well, if you want to have top surgery in the future (removing your breasts for a flatter look), binding for long periods can cause chest tissue damage, making it more difficult. You also need to ensure you wash your binder frequently as they can get super smelly, and cause rubbing and even burns. But at the end of the day, it's up to you how you wear your binder and it's important to weigh up the risks of mental health associated with dysphoria; do what's best and healthy for you. I wear my binder during sex and exercise as I know my limits, but I always pack an extra sports bra to change into whenever I'm out and about in case I need to.*

Tucking

Tucking is the method of concealing the penis to appear flatter... again, we will come back to this. Most folks will flatten their penis and balls and wear tight underwear to keep everything in place whilst others may use special tape or underwear to tuck. However, using medical tape can cause irritation and can make using the bathroom more difficult. Alongside irritation, infections (UTIs), twisting and/or problems with urinating are also risks when tucking. Just as with binding, it's important to take breaks from tucking.

Packing

Packing is the method of creating a bulge near the genital area. This can be achieved by wearing a packer, which could be made from silicone and can appear super realistic, or a foam cup, or rolled-up socks.

Dysphoria

When an individual's expression doesn't align with their gender

---

* My current trans partner can't wear a binder for medical reasons and that can be tough for him – but regardless of whether you bind or not, you're still valid in your gender identity!

identity, this can lead to feelings of dysphoria that we have already spoken about: body, mind and social.

Dysphoria comes in many forms and is individual to each trans person. For example, I experience dysphoria around my chest, which causes me to feel uncomfortable in my body and self – which is why I wear binders to help ease those feelings!

Fem, masc and andro

There are a variety of different types of expressions, but let's have a look at the three umbrella expressions that you may see or even engage with yourself:

Fem – not femme

Fem is an expression which is traditionally feminine – fem individuals play with femininity using stereotypically feminine clothing items, hairstyles, makeup trends and behaviours. Any individual of any gender identity can express themselves in a fem way, and this has zero to do with their gender identity.

This is not to be confused with 'femme', which is a term used specifically within the lesbian community to distinguish feminine lesbians and bisexual women from butch women. I have made this mistake before, using the term 'femme' when I meant 'fem', and it wasn't until an amazing lesbian poet explained to me the origin of the label that I learnt who can use it – we all learn, that's the beauty of our community!

Masc

Masc is short for masculine – appearances that align with stereotypically or socially believed male ways of dressing, wearing their hair and behaving. However, it isn't only men who can appear masc, masc has its own home within queer culture and identity, from masc lesbians who appear butch to masc-leaning gender-diverse folks who prefer a more 'boyish' look.

Andro – short for androgynous/androgyny

Andro or androgynous expression is the in-between of fem and masc expression, taking elements from both expressions to create a gender-neutral look. Androgyny isn't the aim for all nonbinary and gender-diverse people, but for some, appearing gender-neutral and being seen as androgynous can help affirm their identity.

Here I go again, reminding you all that the layers of our identity are fluid and ever-changing, and expression is no different. You are free to explore your identity through your expression, showing the world who you are through your clothes or hair in a way that aligns with a community or identity, or you can simply wear what you personally like. You should never feel like you *must* look a certain way to be part of a certain community; you are still queer, bisexual, nonbinary, gay or straight regardless of how you wear your hair or what shoes you buy!

Body positivity for trans folks

As a trans and gender-diverse+ person, body positivity can be challenging, but it isn't out of reach. For those of us who experience dysphoria, struggle with societal stigma or feel pressure to conform to unrealistic beauty standards or passing standards, loving ourselves can be tricky. Regardless, body positivity is for everyone, and everyone deserves to feel good in themselves and their skin.

What do I mean by passing?

Passing is when someone is perceived as the gender identity they want to be seen as. You may also hear this being called 'passing privilege' as those who aren't perceived as trans may experience less harassment than trans folks who do not pass. Passing is not every trans person's goal.* I for one enjoy being a confusing mess of gender, but I have friends whose goal is to be perceived only as a man or a woman. However, some trans folks feel a pressure to try to pass, believing the misconception that 'passing' means you're a 'successful' trans person. You're a trans person regardless of whether you pass or not, or if you want to or not.

Despite the challenges trans folks experience, there are ways to embrace body positivity that works for **all folks, of all identities**. These include:

- ⊙ Practising self-care – taking care of your physical and mental health can improve your relationship with your body. This may include getting enough sleep, eating well, starting medication, exercising or simply participating in activities you enjoy, such as reading.
- ⊙ Focus on your inner qualities – your worth is not deter-mined by your appearance, you're still you regardless of

---

* My current partner has a love-hate relationship with passing. He wants to pass as a trans man but not as a cis man, for various reasons, and many other trans folks feel the same.

how you look or feel about your body. Think about all the things that make you *you*, your kindness, your humour, your talents etc.

- ◉ Surround yourself with supportive people – finding your tribe and surrounding yourself with people who love you for who you are.
- ◉ Diversifying your feed – are you following folks of all body types? Fat bodies, queer bodies, disabled bodies, Black bodies, Brown bodies, pre-surgery/post-surgery bodies.
- ◉ Be aware of what content you're consuming – what content makes you feel good about yourself, and what doesn't (we will speak more about this in the next chapter!).

Gender equality

Regardless of your gender identity, the fight for gender equality is a fight for every single one of us.

Our gender isn't only about how we feel and navigate the world, it's how others treat us. Gender equality is a fundamental human right, but, unfortunately, society is far from achieving total gender equality globally. When we talk about gender equality, we mean (most of the time) our assigned sex at birth and how that impacts our experience of gender equality. Stereotypes and assumptions about specific gender identities and sex can shape how society treats individuals, and these assumptions hurt all individuals, including trans and nonbinary folks. Where do these assumptions come from? Well, some assumptions and stereotypes have specific origin stories, but in general, they are created by people (our friends and family), through media, literature, religion and culture.

The patriarchy hurts everyone

The patriarchy is a social system where men hold power and women, and non-men (gender-diverse+ individuals), are excluded from it. The patriarchy ensures that men have primary power within roles of political leadership, moral authority, social privilege and control of property. The patriarchy normalizes discrimination and oppression based on sex and gender, which is why all individuals, regardless of their gender identity or sex, can be hurt by the patriarchy. But those who also experience another form of discrimination – LGBTQIA+ individuals, immigrants, folks who are working class, people of colour, specific groups and faiths – may be even more harmed by the patriarchy.

I also want to say that the patriarchy also hurts boys, men and AMAB individuals because it raises them with certain beliefs about themselves. The patriarchy makes it seem that boys and men who share their emotions and feelings, who are sensitive, aren't 'real men'. These beliefs force boys to act in specific ways, forcing them into stereotypes, and those who don't conform are shamed. The patriarchy also can lead to mental health difficulties, from the pressures of not being allowed to share their emotions or seek help when they are struggling, which is why male suicide rates are higher than most other groups.*

---

* In the UK, 74% of all suicides involve men. Generalizing across all cases of suicide is not always helpful, but the main causes of suicide in men relate to the role of men in society, financial difficulties, substance abuse, lack of communication and access to support. See www.ons.gov.uk/peoplepopulationandcommunity/birthsdeathsandmarriages/deaths/bulletins/suicidesintheunitedkingdom/2022registrations

Chapter 6
Beyond Yes and No

Before we get into the ins and outs of going in and out, we need to talk about **consent**.

This chapter is one of the few which I will give a content warning beforehand as we will be talking about rape, sexual assault, abuse and harassment. I totally understand if this chapter is a heavy read, but it is such an important one and I hope I can make this conversation a little easier because consent can be fun and sexy, and we consent to things every single day!

Consent

Consent means freely agreeing to something once you know exactly what you are agreeing to.

When we talk about consent within sex, we mean freely agreeing to all sexual contact. Without consent, sexual acts become sexual assault or rape. Consent is never implied by your past behaviour, what you wear or where you go, and silence is not consent. Consent is the same for all genders and sexualities; regardless of what kind of sex you're having and with whom, consent is a must, and it must follow FRIES!

But before I explain what FRIES is, what I want you to take away from this chapter, if you only take away one thing, is that *you always have the final say with what happens to and with your body.* Your body and space is yours alone, and it is your choice whether or not you invite someone into that space or to touch your body in any way.

What the heck has FRIES got to do with consent?

No, I'm not just thinking of McDonald's fries as I write this chapter (though I do love a good maccies fry). FRIES or F.R.I.E.S. is an acronym created by Planned Parenthood and is used within the sex education world to break down consent:*

F **Freely given** – consent should be given without feeling any pressure, force or manipulation.

R **Reversible** – you can change your mind or withdraw from any form of intimacy at any stage.

I **Informed** – you know exactly what you are agreeing to do with clear language you understand.

E **Enthusiastic** – if you don't give an enthusiastic 'YES!' then it's a no.

S **Specific** – consent is specific for this one situation and cannot be used for future situations (you must obtain consent every single time!).

---

* www.plannedparenthood.org/learn/relationships/sexual-consent

Before we break these down further, let's back-track. As I said before, you consent to things every single day and, guess what, you already know how to obtain and give consent! Can I have the last bag of crisps? Do you want to watch a movie tonight? Would you like to go to this gig next week? Can you empty the dishwasher please? These are all things I said to my partner in the span of an evening and all of them involve consent. We are taught the concept of consent from a very young age, but weirdly we never use that word until we start talking about it in sex, dating, intimacy or touching.

As I said, consent, or lack of consent, is taught to us. We learn consent (or we don't learn consent) based on a variety of factors, mostly what environment we are raised in and by whom. For me, I was taught consent from a very early age by my mum. As soon as I began to explore my own body and to notice that my body was different to other people's bodies, she taught me that no one can touch mine without me allowing them to. That my body was mine only, and with that she taught me that other people's bodies are theirs. However, not everyone I grew up with was taught consent as I was, and I quickly found that out as I went into secondary school. I learnt consent in a general sense way before I knew what sex was, but when I became interested in other people roman-tically and sexually, I didn't know how to use these skills in this new context. That's why understanding consent as a broad topic and understanding sexual consent as a branch within that is vital. It's also important to understand sexual consent in a legal sense too, that's where age of consent comes in.

What is 'age of consent'?

Age of consent is the legal age you can consent to sex. This means you and the person (or people) you are being intimate with must all be of the legal age of consent. This age varies throughout history, from country to country, from state to state in the US, but regardless of where you are, abiding to that legal age of consent is vital. In England and Wales, the age of consent is 16; however, as I said, the legal age of consent varies from place to place, and even as close to England as Ireland is, the age of consent is higher: being 17. In most European countries, the age of consent is between 14 and 16 years of age. Age of consent isn't a goal for when you should be having sex from. It's not that you are expected to have sex the minute you turn 16, not at all! Age of consent is simply when a young person can legally consent to have sex with other people of a similar age. In terms of solo sex, or masturbation, you can do that whenever you feel ready to – some folks start wayyy before they can have partnered sex, some never masturbate, and some young children or even babies masturbate or explore their genitals because it's a part of their body which is exciting and new.

Yes, some people have sex before the age of consent and some people wait!

Many young people have partnered sex before they turn 16 (or whatever age is the legal age of consent where they live). I had sex for the first time at 15 and I know people who had sex a year or so before that. Some people feel ready and prepared to begin experimenting sexually before the legal age of consent. So why is sexual consent set at a specific age if people are having sex before they turn that age? Well, the law is there to protect young people. Sex can come with risk. Sex is never 100 per cent safe; it can be made safer through contraception (which we will come to in Chapter 8), but there are things that can happen outside of our control. The main risks that people worry about when it comes to having sex are sexually transmitted infections (STIs) and/or the risk of unwanted pregnancy. Most STIs are treatable, but many young people may not know whether they have an STI or not (because STIs don't have visible symptoms) and going to a sexual health clinic can be extremely daunting. I remember having to get emergency hormonal contraception (EHC) at 15 because the condom had broken inside me, and I was *terrified* of not only taking myself to the clinic but talking with an adult about what had happened. I felt embarrassed, but also terrified that they would tell me off or arrest me or something (this shows how little sex education I had, I truly believed I would be arrested for having underage sex, even though I had used contraception and tried my best to be safer) – I know first-hand how scary it is to go to a clinic as a young person, which is why many folks simply don't go, regardless of whether the sex was consensual or not.

Having a baby is a huge decision for anyone, let alone a young person. There are also medical complications that can come with teenage pregnancies and births.*

Ok, so can you have sex under the age of consent? The law says you shouldn't have sex under the age of consent, but young people will and have done for as long as 'age of consent' has been a thing, and there is an exception. If both young people are between the ages of 15 and 16 and have healthy consensual sex, then the law recognizes this as an exception – meaning it's legal (aka, Dee at 15 would not be arrested for having consensual sex with

---

* See www.ncbi.nlm.nih.gov/pmc/articles/PMC9859398

their 15-year-old partner). However, if there is any evidence of one person being pressured into having sex, or if there is a large gap between each person (over two years between them with one over the legal age and one under), or if one person is in a position of power over the other, then this becomes way more serious. For some countries and states, the age difference between the two or more people being intimate with one another should not exceed a specified amount.*

Can someone at 16 have sex with anyone over 16/17?
No.

UK law says that 16- and 17-year-olds can legally have sex, but at this age they are also still legally children. If a child has an intimate and sexual relationship with an adult (someone of the age of 18 or over), this is illegal. It is also illegal for an adult in a position of trust or responsibility (such as a teacher or a coach, a councillor) to have a sexual relationship with a 16-year-old – this may be viewed by law as grooming.

> Grooming is when someone builds a relationship, trust and emotional connection with a child or young person so they can manipulate, exploit and abuse them.**

And the same thing goes for paying for sex and explicit photos – it is also illegal to pay for sex with someone 16 or 17 if you are 18 or over; this is not sex work, it is child abuse – and it is illegal to

* www.themix.org.uk/crime-and-safety/your-rights/age-of-consent-9106.html
** www.nspcc.org.uk/what-is-child-abuse/types-of-abuse/grooming

have explicit photos of someone between the ages of 16 and 18; this is child pornography, not consensual pornography.

So even though 16-year-olds can legally have sex, there are still exceptions and laws that protect them.

Can I wait?
Of course!

What about those who wait? Yes, some people wait to have sex for a variety of reasons including faith or simply how they internally feel. Some folks don't want to have sex at all, or it's something that isn't on their to-do list any time soon, whether they are asexual or simply not interested in sex when they hit the legal age. Again, age of consent isn't a 'go go go' for having sex. If you don't want to have sex, either now or ever really, then you don't have to! It really comes down to whether the individual is ready or if they even want to have sex yet. Remember, only you can govern when and if you are ready for sex, so do what feels best and right for you!

Freely given

F is for Freely given; as I said above, this means consent is obtained without pressure or force or manipulation. Consent must be freely given for all forms of sexual activity including kissing, hugging, fingering and/or hand jobs, anal, undressing... anything and everything must have consent behind it.

Who should ask for consent? **Everyone.** It is everyone's responsibility, regardless of their gender, or what role they are playing in the bedroom, to ask for and obtain consent. Generally speaking, the person instigating the sexual act, or suggesting beginning a sexual act, should ask for consent from the other person, but consent works both ways, so both parties (or more if there's more people) should give and ask for consent.*

If someone is drunk, high, asleep or unconscious, they also cannot freely give consent. For consent to be valid, the person must be totally in control of their decision. Only you can consent to engaging in sex with someone else and you must be able to make that decision without external factors like drink or drugs influencing or impacting you.

LET'S TALK ABOUT PRESSURE!

No, I won't sing the line... UNDER PRESSURE... ok, I did! You try saying pressure *without* saying the line!

Peer pressure comes from many different angles, from our friends, our family, our partners, our tribes and society (the worst of the bunch!). And through peer pressure, we are told what we should and shouldn't do, who we should and shouldn't be, what type of sex we should or shouldn't be having. What people around us do on a day-to-day basis influences what we do, and this isn't necessarily always a bad thing. Say you're at your friend's house and they put on a movie that they really love and want you to watch, which you haven't seen before, and you end up loving it. Or you see your local LGBTQ+ community are organizing a community space and all your friends have signed up to help, so you decide to as well so you're not left out, but you end up really enjoying being part of your local LGBTQ+ community. These are examples of good peer pressure. Who we are as an individual also influences the things we are told are ok or not ok for us to do. Our gender, sex, religion, faith, race, body type, disability and

---

* www.brook.org.uk/your-life/consent-and-sex-in-long-term-relationships

education all have their own 'rules' on how we should be as a person, and we choose whether to listen to these rules and influences.

As I said, there's good and bad peer pressure, and the most important thing you remember is that it is always ok to say no if you don't want to do something, you always have the right to choose whether you listen to the influences or not. Especially when it comes to anything sexual or intimate.

HOW DO PEOPLE GIVE AND GET CONSENT?

So, the question is, *how* do people give and get consent? As we've said, consent must be freely given, under no influence, but how do you consent to something or make sure you obtain consent? We've already touched on this slightly but there are a variety of different ways someone can consent to any sexual activity. Consent must be given both verbally and non-verbally – by saying it and showing it.

Verbal consent can be as simple as saying 'yes' to a question such as 'Do you want to have sex?' or 'Do you want to kiss/touch?', but verbal consent can also look like 'Keep going' or 'I like that', phrases and sounds that show you are enjoying the sexual activity and are happy to continue. Asking questions is a great way to obtain consent throughout sex, and it doesn't ruin the mood at all. In fact, asking questions throughout can be super sexy and attractive, it helps to make sure everyone is enjoying what is happening, and if not, things can be changed up or stopped altogether.

Non-verbal consent means the person you're engaging with sexually is showing physically that they are enjoying it with their body language and actions. You can give these non-verbal consent signals to the person you're sleeping with and watch out for them from the person you're engaging with. Some examples of

non-verbal consent include smiling, laughing, reaching for a condom, undressing yourself/themselves, guiding their/your hands
to parts of their body.

WOULD SOMEONE SAY 'YES' WHEN THEY MEAN 'NO'?
This is where the importance of the combination of verbal and
non-verbal consent is important. Some may verbally say 'yes' to
a sexual act but not really mean it. But why would they say 'yes'
then? There are various answers for this, most of which tie into
feeling pressured or worrying about rejecting their partner. Some
folks panic or say 'yes' because they think they are meant to say
yes, particularly if their long-term partner is asking them to do
something that they have previously done before. Remember also
that someone cannot say 'yes' if they are drunk or high or unconscious; even if they verbally say 'yes', it isn't a consensual yes. We
will cover this again at 'E', but a 'yes' must be enthusiastic and it
must be combined with non-verbal consent. If you ever think
someone's 'yes' is unclear, stop and check in with them.

HOW TO SAY 'NO'
So, we've covered how to say yes and show that we are happy
to have sex, but how do we let the person know that we don't
want to have sex or be intimate with them? Saying 'no' can feel
way harder than saying 'yes' and most of that comes down to not
wanting to upset the other person. I'll be the first to admit it, I'm
a huge people-pleaser and I have been known to accept food
from people that I don't want but can't say 'no' to. I've always
struggled to say 'no' to things. I've always found that saying 'yes'
and just dealing with the consequences of my own actions can be
less anxiety provoking and awkward than saying what I want to.

And that's *wrong*. It's something I've been unlearning, and I want to help you to know that you do not need to say 'yes' to *anything* unless you want to!

Setting boundaries can be difficult at first, but as with most things, practice makes perfect. Maybe start setting boundaries outside of sex, like not accepting food that you don't like *Dee*, but seriously, turning things down in everyday life will help you to navigate turning things down in sexual situations. Within the last year, I have become way more confident saying 'no' to things in the bedroom with my partner or 'no' to sex in general. As a trans person, having a voice in the bedroom is key for managing dysphoria, to ensure that I enjoy sex without feeling dysphoric. We will go into more detail about sex for queer and trans folks in the next chapter, but I'll share one example now. Sometimes I dislike my chest and sometimes I love my chest. When I am feeling dysphoric about my chest and we are going to have sex, I will tell my partner that my chest is a 'no go' and he will happily avoid it. This is also coupled by wearing a binder or t-shirt during sex, a non-verbal signal to my partner that I am not comfy with my chest right now.

Just as giving consent can be verbal and non-verbal, saying 'no' can be verbal and non-verbal. Sometimes people will find non-verbal 'nos' easier than saying it. If you're not 100 per cent sure that they are 100 per cent into whatever you're doing or suggesting, stop and talk to them.

WHY DON'T SOME PEOPLE ASK FOR CONSENT?
The most common answer to this is that asking for consent will ruin the mood, or some folks are simply shy or embarrassed, but as we have already touched on, asking questions can be super

sexy and attractive and there is nothing to be embarrassed about when asking for consent! Some folks may have never been taught consent. As I said above, I was lucky enough to be taught consent from a young age, but many people I met in secondary school weren't taught it and many adults to this day aren't taught consent in a healthy and inclusive way. They weren't taught the difference between verbal or non-verbal, or how to ask questions, or FRIES.

LGBTQIA+ CONSENT

For LGBTQIA+ folks, consent within queer relationships or sexual encounters is hardly *ever* touched upon in sex ed lessons, mostly because consent is focused on P in V sex (penis in vagina sex). I think it's important that we talk about the legal definition of rape in the UK:

> The Sexual Offences Act 2003 says that someone commits rape if all of the following happens: They intentionally penetrate the vagina, anus or mouth of another person with their penis. The other person does not consent to the penetration. They do not reasonably believe that the other person consents.*

Sexual assault is defined in a very similar way, with the addition of groping and forced kissing. By this definition, most LGBTQIA+ sexual assault doesn't 'fit', and this is one reason why queer victims do not speak out or do not know that they can and should speak out. Additionally, LGBTQIA+ folks are sadly hypersexualized and stigmatized by society, which has led to higher rates of sexual assault towards queer people compared to their cisgender and

---

*   www.legislation.gov.uk/ukpga/2003/42/contents

heterosexual counterparts.** As society views LGBTQIA+ folks as hypersexual, people assume that LGBTQIA+ people are more sexually active and available, which not only puts queer people in danger of sexual assault but means speaking out about these assaults may fall on ignorant ears. And because of this stigma, LGBTQIA+ folks may hesitate to speak out about sexual harassment or abuse due to fear of discrimination. Some people may also not be 'out' yet, and sharing that they have experienced sexual abuse from someone of the same sex or gender may put them in a dangerous situation or 'out' them before they are ready to share their identity. The reality is that consent is needed in all forms of sex, from all genders and sexualities, even when a penis isn't involved.***

CONSENT WITH THE LGBTQIA+ COMMUNITY

Then there's the other end of the stick, people who know consent is vital but choose to not attain it – this is not only wrong, it's a crime. Some people believe that they do not need to attain consent and will grope, touch, grab people without their consent. This is never, ever ok. I will come back to sexual abuse in a moment, but before we explore FRIES more, it's important that you know that it is never your fault if someone doesn't get your consent and sexually abuses you. Yes, it is everyone's responsibility to ask and obtain consent, but it is never your fault if something happens or is done to you without your consent. Regardless of

---

** https://williamsinstitute.law.ucla.edu/press/ncvs-lgbt-violence-press-release
*** My trans boyfriend will always ask 'are there any nos today?' before we are intimate, and I just *love* that! How simple!

how you identify, sexual assault and abuse is never your fault, though it may feel that way.*

WHAT TO DO IF SOMEONE DOESN'T ACCEPT YOUR 'NO'
If the person/s you're engaging sexually with does not accept your no, you can be firm and repeat yourself. Tell the person/s that if they respect you as a person, they will respect your choices.

IT'S OK TO SAY 'NO', EVEN IF IT'S HARD TO HEAR
It can be hard to hear 'no', particularly from someone you love or for something you want to do or have. Rejection can *suck*. It is totally natural to worry about upsetting or disappointing someone when saying 'no', but it's vital to remember that only you get to decide about your body and what you do and/or what someone else does to it. Sometimes you're going to upset people, maybe even someone super close to you, but they will get over it, and if they don't, they aren't the sort of people you want in your life. You also don't have to explain why you are saying 'no' to someone.

'NO' IS A FULL SENTENCE
No doesn't mean 'maybe', no doesn't mean 'convince me', no doesn't mean 'ask again'. No means no. Your 'no' is important.

You don't have to 'make it up' to someone by doing something else or by apologizing when you say no. You don't need to wait until you really can't take any more of what's happening to say 'no'. You don't have to try something before saying 'no'. You have

---

* I have personally experienced groping or inappropriate behaviour in queer spaces, and challenging these behaviours can feel extremely difficult, but in regards to who has touched you, if you did not/do not want to be touched in that way/by that person, you can speak out.

the power to say 'no' at any point before, during or after sex or intimacy – there is no time frame for saying it.

Now, there are ways to say 'no' without saying... well, no. You can say things like – 'I don't want to do that' or 'I'm not in the mood' or 'That's enough' or 'I'm done now' or 'Stop'.

It's vital to remember that no single verbal or non-verbal signal of consent is enough on its own, and that even if the person is giving these signals, consent can be withdrawn at any point.

Reversible

Consent can be given or taken away at any point. You or the person you're being intimate with may and can change their mind at any stage during intimacy, and once that happens, whatever is happening between the two of you must stop immediately. Consent can be taken away if you're both naked in bed, if you've begun kissing and touching one another, when a condom has been put on, and even when someone is penetrating someone. Just because you have someone's consent once doesn't mean you have their consent always.

Again, it can feel awkward or uncomfortable to say 'no', especially when you've said yes just moments before. But what's more uncomfortable is going through with something you don't want to due to worry or embarrassment. It can also feel awkward to hear a 'no' when you've just heard a 'yes' – but again, you must listen to the person's 'no' and stop immediately.

Consent must be gained before every single sexual act, every single time, even if you're doing something with someone that you've done before. As I said above, as a trans person, some sexual acts are a-ok some days and other days a hard-no – does it mean they are always hard nos? No! Let me explain what I mean by 'hard-nos'. I want to reiterate that 'no means no' and there is no exception to that. But I do think it's important we talk about hard-nos and soft limits and how what we are interested in or wishing to try can change and evolve throughout our sexual experiences. This doesn't mean that our consent is invalid; on the contrary, it reinforces the fact that consent must be obtained for every single unique sexual encounter and act.

- ⊙ A 'hard-no', or a 'hard limit', is a sexual act that you do not want to participate in at all.
- ⊙ A 'soft limit' is something you aren't really interested in but would like to try in the right circumstances or at some stage.

This is *not* to say that when someone says 'no' they mean 'maybe' or 'maybe in the future', it's more to say that getting consent every time you participate in a sexual act is key because what a person wants to try or do may change. We evolve, we grow, we experiment and explore sexually – we are allowed to experiment and explore in a safe way and, for that to happen, consent must always be the top priority.

Informed

You can only consent to something if you have all the facts about that thing – that goes for sex too. When you consent to being intimate with someone, or engaging in a sexual act, you must know all the details about that act, what it involves, what the possible consequences are, and you must be able to say no. A sexual act can go from consensual to non-consensual.

For example, if someone says they will wear a condom

throughout but remove the condom mid-way without you knowing, this is non-consensual. This is called 'stealthing' and is when someone removes a condom or lies about having one on in the first place during sex. Stealthing is rape under English and Welsh law.

Any form of sexual intimacy that occurs without informed consent is sexual assault.

Enthusiastic

No means no – this falls under 'E' in FRIES, as we've already touched on. But what does enthusiastic consent look like? It's more than simply saying 'yes'. Of course, a 'yes' is a must, but the 'yes' must be combined with other verbal and non-verbal signs. An enthusiastic 'yes' can look and sound like many things:

- Literally saying 'yes'
- 'Do that'
- 'Touch me there'
- 'Can you...'
- 'Harder/faster/slower'.

Some other verbal and non-verbal signs may look like:

- Asking permission before you change the type of sexual activity you're doing, using phrases like 'Is this ok?'
- Checking in throughout, saying things like 'Is this still ok?'
- Giggling, laughing, generally having fun
- Talking through the sexual activity, guiding your partner, showing them what to do and giving feedback
- Making eye contact (personally I'm not an eye contact

person, I love closing my eyes and simply enjoying, but I will make eye contact every now and then to let my partner know that I'm a-ok!)

- ⊙ Placing your partner's hands on you/body parts (this also is a good way for showing your partner where on you is an ok place to touch or where isn't)
- ⊙ Biting your lip, winking
- ⊙ Moaning and making noise (of course, not everyone will make noise during sex, and it is *not* a requirement for showing that you're enjoying it or getting off!).

As you can see, enthusiastic consent can look and sound like lots of different things. Coupling verbal and non-verbal signs to show your partner/s that you're enjoying it is a great way of making consent sexy and fun.

Specific

And finally, the S of FRIES – Specific. Saying 'yes' to one thing is *not* saying 'yes' to everyone from now to eternity. A 'yes' is individual for each sexual act, meaning you should ask and give consent multiple times during one sexual activity. This also means that a 'yes' can't be carried over to another sexual activity, on another day – if you say yes to anal sex one evening, you can say no to anal sex another evening.

Gender-based violence (GBV)

We spoke about gender inequality in Chapter 5, and this section falls into that theme, but I think it's important that we cover it in the context of consent. Gender-based violence is a violation of human rights. Gender-based violence is present in every society

BEYOND YES AND NO

around the world, taking many forms, and is rooted in the stereotypes and assumptions we spoke about previously (the idea
that men are strong and powerful whilst women and non-men
are weak and helpless).

Over one third of girls, women and AFAB individuals globally
will experience some form of violence in their lifetime; however,
this figure rises in emergencies, conflict and crisis.* Gender-based
violence can manifest in different ways; some of these include:

- physical violence
- emotional violence
- psychological violence
- femicide (killing of girls, women and non-men)
- sexual violence (rape, sexual assault, coercion)
- female genital mutilation (FGM)
- stalking
- online abuse and harassment
- early and forced marriage (including child marriage)
- denial of resources
- exploitation.

Intimate Partner Violence (IPV)

Also known as 'domestic violence', this is an all-too common form
of violence against girls, women and non-men. IPV refers to any
behaviour from a current or previous partner that causes harm, including physical aggression, sexual coercion, psychological abuse
and controlling behaviours. Globally, the UN reports that one in

---

* www.who.int/news/item/09-03-2021-devastatingly-pervasive-1-in-3-
women-globally-experience-violence

145

four girls, women and non-men have been subjected to violence from an intimate partner at least once in their lifetime.*

Those who are at higher risks of IPV include:

- those with disabilities
- LGBTQIA+ folks
- older women and non-men
- young and adolescent individuals
- ethnic minorities
- refugees and migrants.

Spotting IPV for queer folks in queer relationships can be difficult as conversations around IPV are typically through a heterosexual, cisgender lens, but LGBTQIA+ folks are also victims of IPV. Some LGBTQIA+ people may not be able to report IPV as they may not be out yet, or may fear not being believed because of their identity, which is a reason many folks don't report.

So how can we, as a society, help end violence against girls, women and non-men?

- Teach all individuals consent education and education around GBV and IPV
- Empower girls, women and non-men economically
- Teaching boys and men how to be allies
- Supporting girls, women and non-men in seeking leadership roles and education
- Challenging gender stereotypes and assumptions
- Unpacking the things we believe about gender and how we view society as a whole.

---

* www.who.int/news-room/fact-sheets/detail/violence-against-women

What to do if you have been raped

- ◉ Safety is your first priority – find a safe place, whether that's a hospital, a clinic, a friend's house, somewhere with people. If you are in immediate danger, call the police.
- ◉ It's important to preserve evidence, and that means not showering or washing your clothes or brushing your teeth afterwards – which is extremely difficult, but these pieces of evidence can go a long way to ensuring the police arrest the person who did this to you. Though it is completely 100 per cent your choice whether you report it or not. If you do decide to report it to the police, take a friend or trusted individual with you for support.
- ◉ When you're ready to, it's important to seek a healthcare provider who specializes in this situation to check you over, both for injuries and sexually transmitted diseases. They can provide medication if necessary and emergency contraception too.
- ◉ You may experience flashbacks, PTSD (post-traumatic stress disorder) and depression following the incident; seeking out long-term help such as therapy is a good idea, when you're ready of course.
- ◉ No matter what route to recovery you take, remind yourself that what happened is not your fault. You are not to blame; nothing you did caused this to happen. The person who assaulted you made their own choice. Things will get better.

Sex is meant to be fun, and fun sex includes consent every single time.

Chapter 7
Beyond P in V

Intercourse, fucking, bonking, humping, shagging, love making, to sleep with... it's time to talk about *sex*.

What exactly is sex? Well, sex is many things, it isn't just when a penis enters a vagina like most of us are or were taught in school. This chapter is going to scare those very teachers because we are going into *detail* about sex beyond P in V (penis in vagina). Sex is an umbrella term for a variety of acts which mostly include one or more sets of genitals which are touched (or not touched) in a way that makes the individual feel euphoric and, in some cases, climax or ejaculate. Some sex acts involve a partner, and other sex acts can be performed solo (we call these solo sex acts).

I want to provide you with everything you need to know about sex, things I was never taught and had to learn on my own in adulthood. So, we are going to go into detail about sex, sexual acts, solo sex and pleasure because why wouldn't we! When I was researching for this book, I found that many sources started with safer sex practices, but most interestingly STIs (sexually transmitted infections – we now avoid the term disease). Most books didn't start with pleasure, or how sex works. Yes, talking about safer sex practices is vital and we will cover that in this chapter, but I want to remind you all that sex is fun. I also wanted to provide you with the information I wish I had been given and shown as a young person, the part that we sadly don't talk about and often find ourselves going to unsafe sites (rhymes with morn-bub) to see, that is the act of sex itself.

When (and really if) you received sex ed in school, you would have learnt about the act of sex but never pleasure – it's one of the most neglected parts of sex ed within the school curriculum. Why? Because some people believed that if we teach young people that sex can be pleasurable, and that you can have sex purely to feel good, that everyone will be fucking, and importantly, fucking in unsafe ways. This just isn't the case. Because at the end of the day, young people will have sex if they want to, regardless of whether we teach it in a way that promotes pleasure or not.

So strap in, and strap on.

The act of sex

As I said, there are a variety of ways to have sex, but let's start with partnered sex.

I want to say that when I say partnered sex, I don't just mean two people. Partnered sex can include two or more people. We will go into more detail about different relationships and how they may look, but keep this in mind!

But first... boundaries!

Before you have *any* form of it, it's important to talk to your partner or person/s you're having sex with about boundaries. We

touched on boundaries in our consent chapter, but it's important to reiterate the importance of communication. Telling the
person/s that you're going to have sex with what you like, what
you dislike, what works for you and what doesn't will *only* lead
to better sex, for everyone involved. However, even after you've
chatted about what you like, what you don't like, you still may
find yourself feeling uncomfortable during sex for a variety of
reasons – this is where a 'safe word' comes in handy.

A safe word is a word you say to stop whatever sexual act is
happening. Once this word is said, everyone stops what they are
doing, and you can either continue with something else or stop
the entire sex session altogether. But before you can use a safe
word, you must decide on one together. It must be a word you
can say super easily but something that isn't too long or that you
would say in the bedroom. Lovehoney, a sex toy company, found
through a study of 1300 people that the most common safe word
was 'red', like the traffic light. Followed by 'pineapple', 'banana',
'orange' and 'peach' – very fruity.*

I personally have always used 'pineapple'. Why? I truly cannot tell you where it came from or why, it just works. Your safe
word is for you to choose; find something that feels right to use,
something you feel comfortable and confident in using during
sex. And even if someone hasn't used a safe word, remember what
we said in the previous chapter – even if someone consents to sex
through verbal and physical signals, if they look uncomfortable,
stop and talk.

---

* www.lovehoney.com/blog/most-popular-safe-words.html

Vaginal and anal penetration
(with a penis, a strap on, a dildo or a vibrator)

It isn't only heterosexual couples who have penetrative sex. Anyone, of any gender, of any sexual orientation, can enjoy and engage with penetrative sex. And I don't mean just P in V sex, I mean toys in vaginas, penises in butts toys in butts, and fingers in holes.

How does penetration work? Well, to have penetrative sex, the penis or the toy must be erect. For a penis owner, this means the person must be turned on, and if you're using a toy, you must use a toy made for penetrative sex – don't worry, we will have a look at sex toys in a bit!

Vaginal sex and the G spot

Vaginal sex isn't just a case of going in and out – there are several ways to make penetrative sex different and unique each time, or for each individual person. One person may prefer slow and steady, another may like fast and deep, and another may like a variety of speeds and tempos. The right positions also play a role in vaginal sex – again, every person is different and may like one position over another. For some folks, they may simply not be able to have sex in specific positions because of their disabilities. Finding what works for you and the person you're having sex with is vital, and it may take some trial and error, some figuring out and lots of communication – but this is totally normal! What porn leaves out most of the time is the detailed conversations that happen between the people involved where they talk through positions, angles, tempos and boundaries. Talking is at the core of having great sex, so don't be shy!

Anal sex and the P spot/G spot

Anal sex involves either a penis, toy or finger penetrating the... well, anus to hit the P spot (the prostate). When it comes to anal sex, starting small is key because: 1. The butt doesn't self-lubricate (see below), and 2. The anal passage has thinner walls than the vagina and this means for penetration to work (and work safely) you got to go slow and gentle, otherwise you may tear. Working your way up to penetration with a penis or a toy may take a few minutes, it may take several different sexual encounters with each exploring the next size up. There isn't a timeline for how fast or slow you should go when trying anal sex and different sizes. It's about listening to the individual's body (and butt). Communication is vital during anal, not only because you can easily hurt yourself, but because having anal sex can make folks feel a little vulnerable, especially if it's someone's first time or if the individual is a penis owner.* Some folks may also never be able to use a toy or penis, that's also totally ok!

Is anal sex messy?
First, all sex can be messy. When there's liquids and bodily

---

* Why would a penis owner feel more vulnerable having anal sex? And why would they want to have anal sex? Unfortunately, there is a lot of misconception and stigma around penis owners who enjoy anal sex, primarily the belief that enjoying anal sex makes you gay. First, this just isn't true. Enjoying specific sexual acts doesn't make you gay, only you as an individual can label yourself. Straight men, straight penis owners can enjoy anal sex. Secondly, all penis owners have a P spot – the prostate gland – which plays a role in producing semen and propelling the semen out the penis when someone cums. However, it also plays a role in anal sex. When the P spot is stimulated, it can feel very pleasurable and even produce orgasms for some folks.

functions involved, yeah, it isn't the prettiest, certainly not what it looks like in porn (more on that in a later chapter!). But yes, anal sex can be messy and is messier than vaginal or other forms of sex. The anus is part of the digestive tract, forming the passage where your waste leaves your body but poop is not stored in this passage. But as poop travels through the passage, there may be small particles left over... meaning you may get some on yourself or a toy, but hey, that's totally ok and natural. If there is ever poop and you don't know what to do, try not to panic. Remove yourself or the toy from the anus, remove the condom, tie and place in tissue paper, wipe yourself with wipes or a towel (Dee's top tip: always keep tissues or wipes near you during sex but especially during anal sex) and hop in the shower. If you're the one who has... well left some waste on someone's penis or toy, don't be embarrassed – it happens! If it happens, it happens.

Now, what if you poop during anal sex? Anal penetration can make you feel like you need to go to the toilet, it makes sense, right, because you're being explored in an area that usually only

> **Myth:** 'Only gay men have anal sex.' No, it isn't only gay cisgender men who have anal sex. As I said, anal sex isn't related in any way to your sexuality, but yes, some gay men have anal sex, but not all do! Some gay men prefer oral, or hand-sex, or preferring penetrating rather than receiving – either way, these are all valid forms of sex.**

** I know plenty of cisgender, straight men who enjoy a little anal play and I personally love anal sex. It's totally down to your personal preference and whether you feel comfortable engaging in that form of sex with someone else. If you don't, or want to explore anal pleasure in private, go for it! Just remember plenty of lube.

sees action when it's time to poop. But if you do poop during sex, here's what you can do:

- Remove and discharge the condom as you would normally do (in the bin).
- Clean yourself up with tissues or towels that are nearby (it's always a good shout to keep tissues and towels at arm's length during sex).
- Have a deep clean as soon as possible, jumping in the shower or bath.
- Once you're clean, and if you feel comfortable enough, have a chat with your partner/s about what happened.
- Make a plan for how to avoid it happening again next time – such as not repeating the same positions or drinking more water or using the loo before you get intimate.

Does sex hurt?

Sex should never be painful... unless you want it to be. Yes, some people enjoy rougher, and even sometimes painful, sex, but even rougher sex needs consent and boundaries. You should also not be in pain during or after sex. Sex can be uncomfortable for your first time, or even after you've been having sex for a while, usually this can be helped by changing positions, using toys or incorporating more lube. However, some folks struggle with having penetrative sex. Most vagina owners say that they have experienced painful sex. And most of us are raised with the fear of having sex for the first time as we have been conditioned to believe that it will hurt. But I'm here to tell you, vagina owners, penis owners, sex should never be painful (again, unless you want it to be) and we shouldn't have to 'put up with it' being painful because we think that's what we are supposed to do.

There are a variety of reasons why sex may be painful or comfortable, and most of these reasons can be solved or helped, as I already suggested above (more lube, changing positions, using toys etc). Did you know that one in six people are allergic or sensitive to latex and condoms but obviously don't know this until they try using one? They may then just think that the pain and how uncomfortably they feel when using a condom is 'normal' because they've always experienced it and continue to use condoms, repeating the cycle, when they should try latex free condoms. When it comes to all things sex, trial and error is key; sex is never perfect and it's ok if we need time to figure out what works for us, but painful sex should never be disregarded as 'normal'.

Some people with vaginas have something called vaginismus which is when the vaginal muscles involuntarily or persistently contract when they attempt vaginal penetration.* This contraction can be extremely painful and can prevent penetrative intercourse. The skin around the vulva can also be sensitive and painful and some vagina owners even struggle to use tampons. For those with vaginismus, sex therapy can be a great way of taking back control when it comes to sex and finding out what kind of sex works for you and the kind you want to be having, but you can also speak to your doctor too.

What about our peen owners? Penis owners can also experience pain during sex, whether it's due to a lack of lube, or a tight foreskin, small cuts on the skin or, as I said, an allergy to latex;

---

* www.circlehealthgroup.co.uk/health-matters/womens-health/vaginismus-painful-sex-and-social-stigma

there are ways to resolve these issues. Some penis owners may also hurt themselves during sex because they are doing it too hard, too quickly, without enough lube, causing a friction burn or even tearing. And in the rarest of cases, yes, a penis can fracture. No, a penis will not break if the person it is inside of sneezes, but if there is significant trauma to an erect penis... it can fracture. It isn't only the responsibility of the one being penetrated to ensure that sex isn't painful, it's everyone's responsibility. If you have a bigger penis, it's important that you use plenty of lube. You may also want to go extra slow and ease into penetration; this will also stop you from tearing.

What's the best way to avoid painful sex? Communication! Talking with the person you are having sex with is the best way to avoid experiencing pain during sex and stopping if something is painful. If at any point sex hurts, you can use your safe word to stop whatever is happening – 'Red!', 'Pineapple!', 'Lemongrass!'

The wetter, the better!

When it comes to penetrative sex, lube is a must. Lube helps the penis, the toy or even your fingers to enter whichever hole you're penetrating as it reduces friction, which makes having sex way more comfortable, fun and safer as it reduces the risk of injury to either person. The anus doesn't self-lubricate, meaning you *must* use lubricant when entering it, otherwise it can be extremely painful and even damaging. The vagina, on the other hand, does self-lubricate when an individual is turned on, but this isn't the case for every vagina owner, particularly for older folks, which is why you should still use lube. You should apply lube before penetration, but also throughout! There's no specific number of times that you can or should apply lube during sex, it's more of a use when and if you need it kind of deal. Now we are talking about lube, I should probably mention all the wonder varieties of lube out there:*

- ◉ **Water-based:** Good for all toys and safe to use on condoms but can be sticky.
- ◉ **Oil-based:** Long-lasting, meaning you won't need to re-apply as often. However, they cannot be used with latex condoms as they may tear.
- ◉ **Silicone-based:** Another long-lasting formula, which is safe to use with all condoms. Unfortunately, it cannot be used with toys as it can degrade them.
- ◉ **Hybrid:** This is a mix of water-based and silicone/oil. Again, super long-lasting and easy to clean off. These can be used with toys.

Oral sex

Oral sex is when you use your mouth, tongue and lips on some-one's ins and outs, but there are different types of oral sex.

Cunnilingus

This is the official name for 'eating someone out' or 'going down on someone' and it's when you lick or suck an individual's vulva or clitoris or bottom growth. There are many ways to do this and

---

* For those with sensory issues like me, finding the lube that is right for you is key. I personally struggle with sticky lubes, so I try to avoid them. But if it's something that cannot be avoided, having someone else apply the lube for you so you don't have to touch it is a great tip.

various techniques that differ from person to person. You can use your entire tongue, or just the tip, you can kiss the labia, or use a combination of tongue and fingers.* There is also so much that you can focus on when it comes to giving oral sex to a vulva owner. You can focus on the clitoris, the labia, their vaginal opening or even the skin around the vulva; going onto the thighs can be a fun place to explore with your tongue.

Blowjobs

No, you do not actually blow on a penis; believe me, we have all thought this before we learnt what a blowjob *really* was. A blowjob, known also as 'head' or 'giving head', or 'fellatio', which sounds very mature to me, is when you use your mouth, lips and tongue on an individual's penis. For trans men with bottom growth, they too can receive head in a very similar way.

However, you can also give a blowjob on a toy... but why would you? There's no sensation for the toy? Well, someone may use a toy or a strap-on (this is when a penetrative toy is attached to a person's hips via a harness) during sex where a penis owner isn't present or isn't using their penis. And to get in the mood, one person may suck the strap-on of the other person, and though this doesn't cause the strap-on wearer pleasure via the strap-on... as it isn't their own body, it still may turn them on. Trans men or trans masculine folks may use a strap during sex and the act of getting head can be super affirming for them, as if the strap is their own penis.

---

* I'll let you into a secret, until 2023 I hadn't ever given a vulva owner head before and I was a tad intimidated by it. However, I can confirm that if you communicate with the person that you're giving head to, you'll figure out what works for them and you. And no, I haven't got lock jaw yet!

Rimming

Rimming is when you lick around an individual's anus; you can also insert your tongue into their rectum too or use a combination of fingers and tongue.

Let's answer some quick-fire questions that I know you're all begging to ask:

Do people even like giving oral sex?

Yes! Some folks do, and some folks don't, it's all down to personal preference, and it's totally up to you whether you give oral or not.

Do your teeth get in the way?

Yes, they can, but like all forms of sex, practice makes it better (not perfect as sex is *never* perfect, and that's the joy of it!). Communicating with the person you're giving head can help you to figure out what works and what doesn't.

Can you get pregnant from a blowjob?

Nope.

Should I use a condom for oral?

Yes! Barrier methods such as condoms should be used even when pregnancy isn't a possibility. We will come back to safer sex practices and protection in the next chapter.

Hand jobs

Hand jobs, also called 'wanking' or to 'wank', is a term for using your hand to touch your own penis or another person's penis. We have already spoken about how a penis gets 'hard' or erect and how it can ejaculate, and a hand job is when an individual will make upwards and downwards movements on an erect penis to make the person or themselves feel good and maybe even ejaculate. Before you get anywhere near another person's penis, it's vital to get consent. The speed or grip that you have whilst giving a hand job may differ from person to person and from time to time; some folks enjoy going slow and others prefer more pressure and a faster pace. It's important to talk to the individual you are giving a hand job to to figure out what they want and like, and to let them guide you.

Fingering

Fingering is a slang term for using your fingers to stimulate a person's vulva, vagina or anus. Fingering doesn't only consist of penetrating, you can use your fingers to touch, stroke, tap the outside of the genitals. Before we get to how to finger, it's important to always ensure your hands, fingers and fingernails are clean before fingering yourself or someone else. It's also vital to check to make sure you do not have any cuts or wounds on your fingers as this can lead to cross contamination. If you want, you can use a finger-cot (a very small finger condom which you can use when fingering someone).

Now for the actual fingering: take it nice and easy, slow and steady, this isn't a race! It's important that you don't go straight to penetrating; penetration feels more pleasurable and is way safer when the individual is relaxed and wet (or, if you're fingering an anus, you have plenty of lube on your fingers and on the anus as the anus doesn't self-lubricate!). You can move your fingers in a variety of ways to make the person feel good, but the most common finger movement is a *'come to me'* kind of movement where you use your index finger and curl in towards you and back again. Also don't forget the

> **Myth:** Have you ever heard of the rumour that if someone sneezes whilst your finger is inside them, it can break your finger? I certainly have and I believed it for many years when I was first sexually active (I actively would avoid sneezing at all costs during sex). Well, this is fake news. A vagina cannot snap a finger or a penis – so if you need to sneeze, please sneeze.

clitoris – we spoke a lot about this gem in the previous chapter and it's important we give it the time it deserves when fingering someone or ourselves! Each person will enjoy different types of touches or speeds, at different times. It's all about adapting and listening. Listen to the person you are fingering – as you're not the one being fingered, you need to listen to the person who is being fingered as they can guide you and let you know what feels good, what doesn't, and whether you need to stop or not.

To avoid pregnancy, it's important to avoid inserting fingers or anything into a vagina that has wet semen on it, and if you are changing between touching yourself and touching someone else that you clean your hands each time or change finger-cots. This also can help avoid transmitting an STI from one to another.

'I'm masturbating. I told you I'd be doing that all day today!'

Masturbating (solo or mutual) is when you touch yourself (solo sex act) or you touch yourself whilst your partner/s touch themselves at the same time. You may have heard it called choking the chicken, wanking, jacking off, tossing off, rubbing one out or touching yourself. Why do people masturbate? Well, there's a few reasons for this. The most obvious one is that it makes people feel good. Masturbation can also relieve sexual tension and reduce stress and can help people to figure out what they want and like so they can tell their partner or future partners what works for them. Solo sex is also great for building confidence and for learning to love your body (as well as to get to know your body on a 1:1 basis).

Masturbation is utterly natural. Did you know that animals also masturbate? Monkeys, whales, elephants, bats, dolphins, turtles all masturbate!

For a lot of trans folks, masturbation can be tricky, pre or post gender-affirming surgery, as it can cause a lot of dysphoria; however, for others it may be the only way they want to engage in sex. Some trans folks will avoid penetration/penetrating as it can induce dysphoria, so masturbation may be the only option they have to achieve pleasure either solo or mutually. *Trans individuals are just as worthy of pleasure as cisgender folks* and many trans individuals have found ways to avoid dysphoria when masturbating. Masturbating is 100 per cent normal, regardless of what body parts you have or how you do it. I have struggled with masturbation and sex since coming out as trans, but there are ways to still rock your socks off without feeling horrible about it or yourself. Here's some of my own tips for avoiding dysphoria whilst masturbating:

- ⊙ Masturbate under a blanket; this way you don't need to see your genitals and can just enjoy the feeling
- ⊙ Wear affirming clothing whilst masturbating, whether

that's a binder, or tucking pants, or a packer
- Buy toys that affirm your identity – that way you don't have to touch your own genitals
- Watch porn which affirms your identity whilst masturbating.

Myth: Can you masturbate too much? There isn't a set number of times or length of time you should be masturbating for. If you are masturbating to a point where it is painful, or you can't stop masturbating and it's impacting your daily life, then it is a good idea to speak to your doctor.

Some folks don't masturbate and that is also completely valid. It's your body and it's your choice whether you want to masturbate. You can also masturbate at any age, there isn't a time limit – yes, older folks masturbate too!

Sex toys 101

Some folks use sex toys to increase their pleasure during sex, some folks use sex toys as the main source of pleasure during sex. It's important to use toys that are designed to be safe, using them specifically for what they are designed for, and to keep them clean. It's also great to find toys that affirm your identity, such as buying a strap-on or packer if you're a trans man. Here are some sex toys on the market, but there are so many unique toys out there to explore and try if you want to:

Vibes/vibrators
As indicated by their name, these are toys that vibrate and these vibrations (of varying levels and intensities) cause stimulation. Vibrators can be used on the clitoris, vulva, penis, scrotum, nipples

and anus – they are a gender-full toy for all identities and sexualities. Other types of vibrators include finger vibrators, pants that vibrate, rabbit vibrators, hands-free/remote control.

Dildos

These toys are shaped like a penis and can come in varying sizes, shapes and veins. Dildos are used primarily for penetrating the vagina or anus, but they can also be used for external stimulation and oral sex. Anyone of any sexuality can be penetrated with a dildo and it has zero to do with their sexual orientation. Other types of dildos include double-ended, realistic, vibrating dildos.

Butt-plugs

These are toys that are inserted into the rectum. These cause pleasure through the feeling of fullness in the anus, or by hitting the P spot for men and AMAB individuals.

Strap-ons

These are harnesses which hold a sex toy onto your body, such as a dildo or packer, which can then be used for penetration. Anyone of any gender can wear a strap and penetrate someone else.

Packers

As I said above, these are like dildos and are used to create the feeling of having a penis (see Chapter 5 for more discussion about packers).

Cock-rings

These are rings that go... well on your penis. They reduce the blood flow, which can help folks maintain an erection for longer, or even make the erection harder.

Speaking of sexual desire...
What about 'sex drive'?

This phrase relates to someone's desire to have sex, but the 'official' term would be libido. One of the biggest sexual organs everyone has is the brain; that baby is in control of everything and determines whether we have sex – even if our body wants it, it's the brain that gets the final say. Many sex educators (including myself) have moved away from the phrase 'sex drive' as it suggests we need sex to survive, and as we discussed, we don't! 'Sex drive' suggests that sex is as important as food, or water, or warmth, and this can push people to engage in sexual activities that they do not want to because they are pressured to do so and make people think they can demand sex from others. Only you can decide if you have sex, and if anyone ever uses the 'but I need it' or 'it's part of human nature' – bin them.

Some folks may have a 'higher sex drive' or a 'high libido', which means they feel like having sex more often, whilst others may have a 'lower sex drive' or a 'low libido'. Regardless of where your libido sits on the scale of always horny to not ever horny, you are valid in your feelings and your feelings should always be respected by your partner/s. The libido is something that exists... say it with me... on a spectrum. Some folks always experience a high libido, or a similar libido level, throughout their life, whilst others may go through changes of horniness. Your libido is also subject to change depending on a variety of factors, both long-term and short-term. Your wellbeing, your menstrual cycle, mental health, your lifestyle choices and medication can all impact your desire to have sex.*

---

* At the time of writing this book I am one week on antidepressants (go

P in V isn't the end goal

As you can see, there is a *lot* more to sex than P in V, but sadly, this idea is still pushed onto a lot of young people and non-penetrative heterosexual sex is not thoroughly taught about in schools. I was never taught about queer sex in school and only truly learnt more about it during my early 20s (lockdown provided a lot of free time for learning and my google search history was messy!) – but this shouldn't be what individuals have to do! We shouldn't have to teach ourselves in our own time... but that's a conversation for another time. Because I didn't receive inclusive sex education, I was extremely anxious when engaging sexually with anyone who didn't have a penis. I couldn't imagine sex without a penis involved and I want to make sure that y'all can.

Penis in vagina sex *isn't* the goal for everyone and it *isn't* the only form of sex. We've already deep dived into a variety of other sexual acts that do not include a penis or penetration, but unfortunately, these sexual acts are seen as 'foreplay' and not the 'main event'. 'Foreplay' is a term used to describe acts that take place before penetration and this term reinforces the idea that

---

me for finally taking the plunge) and I was prepared for my sexual desire to fluctuate because of the medication. I have always been a high libido girlie, always being the more sexually active partner in a relationship, spending most of my eves masturbating before bed (which is totally ok!). However, my libido disappeared, vanished, the week I began antidepressants, and as I'm writing this section, I haven't had sex in nine days (a new record for me). Will I have sex again? Yeah, my body is just adjusting to the medication. Is it fascinating what medication can do to your desire for sex? *Totally!* Your libido may go for a while and then come back in full force – if your desire for sex has dipped, that's totally ok. If you have concerns about it, chat with your doctor. Hopefully, by the time you're reading this book, I have returned to my horny self. (I'll keep you posted.)

penetration is the 'main event'. I do not use the term 'foreplay' for this very reason as it invalidates other forms of sex – I prefer to use the terms 'outercourse' and 'intercourse'. Outercourse refers to any sexual act that doesn't include penetration, and intercourse describes any sexual act that involves penetration (which isn't limited to a penis in a vagina).*

Pee after sex... all kinds of sex!

It is good to pee after sex, after all forms of sex, but specifically after P in V sex to prevent bacteria entering the urethra and causing a UTI. I pee after solo sex. Why? Because it just feels right to – it's down to personal preference, but peeing after sex is a good way to flush anything out, and as I said, to keep bacteria away. If you've had anal sex, you should also pee, and you may find that you also need to poop. Which is totally normal (and understandable as you've just had something inside your butt), and it's important to keep in mind that if you do poop, it may be a different texture or smell compared to your usual.**

Vanilla is a good flavour!

You might have heard of 'vanilla sex' before and people using it as an insult, but I'm here to say that vanilla sex is just as valid as

---

* As I said previously, I am in my first T4T relationship and I'm engaging in more sex that isn't penis centred, because neither of us have one, and I'm *loving it*. Since being intimate with another vulva owner, I have seen sex in a totally different way. Sex without a penis is *just as valid* as sex with one.
** I once was intimate with someone who after sex said 'Dee, you need to pee' and it was honestly so romantic.

any form of sex. Vanilla sex refers to sex that is 'conventional' – now what does that really mean? It means folks who have sex in missionary, one person on top, one on the bottom, and that's about it. Does having sex in one position mean you're boring? Nope, you just know what you like! Some folks don't want or need loads of toys, or changing up positions, or role play to truly enjoy sex, and there is no room for kink shaming or sex shaming! Whether you like vanilla, chocolate, mint or bubble-gum, your interests and desires in the bedroom are valid (if they are consensual).

O is for Orgasm

La petite mort: 'A little death'.

This French phrase is sometimes used to describe the feeling after an orgasm. Orgasms are the release of built-up physical and/or psychological sexual tension and arousal. In other words, it's an intense sensation of sexual pleasure that builds up during sexual acts. You may also know it by 'cumming', or 'coming', or 'climaxing'. An orgasm is created by the tensing and releasing of certain muscles, which is then followed by ejaculation and a release of feel-good hormones which makes us feel relaxed and pleased.

For those with a penis, whilst being erect, your testicles will also move closer to your body as the skin around them (the scrotum) gets tighter. Your testicles will also enlarge as more blood flows to the area, your thighs and buttock muscles tense, your blood pressure rises, and your pulse quickens. On average, an orgasm for penis owners lasts 10–30 seconds. After you have reached climax, penis owners are unable to orgasm again right away. This is called the 'refractory period', and the length of this period varies from person to person, lasting between a few minutes to a few days and it is totally normal. This period also will become longer as you become older.

For those with a vulva and vagina, your heart rate and blood pressure increases, your chest may increase by as much as 25 per cent and your nipples may become erect. The pelvic floor muscles will contract around every 0.8 seconds. On average, an orgasm for a vulva and vagina owner lasts between 31 and 51 seconds and most vagina owners do not have a refractory period, meaning they can orgasm again very soon after. These are known as 'multiple orgasms'.

However, not everyone will orgasm or be able to orgasm – though that's not what society or porn teaches us.

The orgasm gap

In 2017, a study which explored orgasm rates between heterosexual men and gay men, bisexual men and lesbian and bisexual women highlighted an issue called 'the orgasm gap' (I'm using the language of the study here).* Folks of all genders orgasmed 95 per cent of the time when engaging in solo sex (masturbation), whilst the numbers were drastically different for partnered sex. Gay men orgasmed 89 per cent of the time, bisexual men 88 per cent and lesbians 86 per cent, whilst heterosexual women and bisexual women only orgasmed 65 per cent of the time. Meaning this issue is a social one, not a biological one. However, the orgasm gap can

* Frederick, D.A., St John, H.K., Garcia, J.R. & Lloyd, E.A. (2018) 'Differences in orgasm frequency among gay, lesbian, bisexual, and heterosexual men and women in a U.S. national sample.' *Archives of Sexual Behaviour* 47, 1, 273–288. https://pubmed.ncbi.nlm.nih.gov/28213723

impact anyone with a clitoris and vagina. But why is that? There are a few reasons: the lack of education around AFAB anatomy and pleasure, inequality in the bedroom, and expectations around sex.

Disabled folks have sex too

Disabled individuals, whether born with a disability or who have acquired a disability throughout their life, can have a fulfilling sex life like anyone else. Sadly, in-class sex education has historically neglected and disregarded disabled individuals, leaving many unsure of whether they can even have sex and unable to protect themselves during sex (i.e. no resources on contraception for disabled bodies). Disabled individuals have been portrayed as asexual or simply unable to have sex in most areas of media, until more recently when shows such as *Sex Education* began to change that narrative, but sadly the misconception is still rife. Disabled individuals are also oversexualized online, they are fetishized by individuals who want to have sex or be intimate with disabled people purely because they are disabled. The reality is that we have failed disabled individuals when it comes to talking about sex and showing them that they too can have a fulfilling sex life if they want one, and when you realize that anyone can acquire a disability, whether physical or mental throughout their life, we are doing a disservice to everyone. As with all sex ed, everyone needs to have insight and information for all forms of sex, with different body types, identities, disabilities, because we may either identify in that group, or date someone who does, or find ourselves in that group later in life.

Those who are disabled may have to think more about the

sex they are having, the logistics of it, and the prep/aftercare they need with whoever they are being intimate with. This may include:

- What positions are possible and most comfortable
- Incorporating breaks throughout
- Checking your blood pressure
- Having something sweet next to the bed in case you need it
- Keeping medication nearby.

I've been with partners who have had chronic back pain and sometimes it was hard to stay in certain positions for long. This was an easy thing for us to monitor and meant that, when they were in a flare up, we could change positions and keep going if we wanted to. As with all forms of sex, these conversations can be fun and sexy and, importantly, ensure you have better sex.

Neurodivergent sex

For those who are neurodivergent or have mental health conditions or learning difficulties, there are also ways to make sex more accessible and comfortable. As someone who experiences sensory overload, sex can be difficult at times, so here are some things to consider when having sex as a neurodivergent individual:

- Your desire in sex may fluctuate, and that's a-ok!
- Novelty is great! Some folks may get bored of the same thing, so changing things up in the bedroom can be a great way to ensure everyone is engaged with what is happening.

This may mean changing positions frequently, trying a new toy or kink, or laying music.

◉ Sensory issues are real! From the smell of lube, the feeling of lace, the touch of someone or orgasming, these can all be a lot for someone which can put them off sex and make them uncomfortable. It's important to be patient with yourself, to talk with your partner about what things may trigger your senses and how to avoid them. Try a new lube outside of the bedroom to see which you prefer or ask your partner/s to not touch certain places on your body for example.

◉ If you're on medication, you may experience lows in desire for sex (aka exactly what I'm experiencing) and that's ok. Being honest about this with your partner/s is vital. You can also talk with your doctor about changing your dose if that's something you're considering.

◉ If you go non-verbal, creating signs to communicate with your partner/s is vital for your safety.

Queer sex is sex

My goal throughout this book has been to ensure that queer experiences are heard and seen in all areas, sprinkled throughout, but I also think it's important to dedicate time to talk specifically about queer and trans experiences. As we have explored, sex isn't just P in V, the penis isn't the centre of the world and not everyone will be having the same sex, yet, unfortunately, there is still this misconception that queer sex isn't 'real sex'. All sex is real sex, whether it's hand-stuff, mouth-stuff, penetrative with toys – it's sex.

Let's debunk some queer sex myths:

> **Myth:** 'Scissoring is real!' – Well, sorry to break it to you, but no, 'scissoring' isn't real, it's actually called tribbing or humping.
>
> **Myth:** 'Lesbians don't get STIs!' – Regardless of your sexuality, or gender identity, you may get an STI throughout your lifetime if you're skin-to-skin or genital-to-genital with someone.
>
> **Myth:** 'All queer sex is kinky!' – Nope, some queer folks enjoy and engage only with vanilla sex. Kinky isn't tied in any way to sexual identity, though queer folks may experiment with kinky more than heterosexual folks.

Having sex as a trans person

Navigating sex as a trans person can be difficult. Managing gender and body dysphoria, possibly whilst managing libido changes due to medication, can add extra anxiety when it comes to having sex. You are in control of whether you have sex, and for some trans people, sex in general, or certain acts or positions, is not possible. Having conversations with your partner/s is vital, discussing what positions make you feel most euphoric, what toys are ok to use, what body parts are ok to touch and how. It's also important to remember that this may change either during one session or from day to day. Checking in with your trans partner/s is important.

Some trans folks may need to wear gender-affirming clothing during sex to feel more comfortable. I have worn my binder during sex, and it's allowed me to engage fully with what's going on without worrying about my chest (plus I feel way sexier with it on!). Folks may want to pack during sex, or wear a strap, or a chest plate, or a wig, whatever gender-affirming item will make them feel more comfortable in themselves whilst being intimate.

When it comes to language in the bedroom, some trans folks

may prefer their genitals being referred to by unique nicknames. This can help avoid dysphoria that may come with biological terms for genitals, and creating a unique name for your genitals to use during sex can be fun. Some trans folks use phrases like 'girl-dick' or 'bussy'; I personally like 'boy-pussy' – Mum, please don't read this, thanks![*, **]

Mind your business!

It's important that we understand that not everyone will engage in sex in the same way that we do or will engage in sex at all.

Sex isn't for everyone. Some folks simply don't want to have sex either solo or with others; these folks may identify as asexual. Not wanting to engage in sex, whether that's on one occasion or ever, is totally normal and should always be accepted. No means no. (See Chapter 4 for a more detailed discussion about attraction types.)

There is also this misconception that certain groups of people are 'sex crazy', mostly boys, men and AMAB individuals, and that girls, women and AFAB individuals aren't that into sex – but that isn't always the case. Everyone's interest in sex differs, and everyone's libido is valid and should be respected.

---

* Whilst writing this book I am in my first T4T relationship and it really has changed how I view sex. One of the most wholesome moments from our very first time being intimate was counting down from three and both showing each other our chests (which are a source of dysphoria for both of us). It was the first time I was intimate with someone who understood *exactly* how I felt about my chest and didn't need educating on what dysphoria was. I will always cherish this memory.

** My trans boyfriend uses a variety of terms to describe his genitals, ranging from dick, to T-dick, to vulva and clit.

Sex isn't only for reproduction. Yes, some folks have sex to procreate, but others have sex simply because they want to. Some folks have sex with folks they can't conceive with (queer relationships/sex) and most folks will use contraception to ensure that they can't get pregnant. And no, it isn't only when 'two people love each other very much...' As I said, you can have solo sex and that doesn't involve another person you 'love', just yourself, but sex doesn't have to be a romantic thing – some folks have sex purely for pleasure, without romantic ties (these people may identify as aromantic). Some folks may engage in 'flings' or 'one-night stands' with people who they may never see or sleep with again, and others prefer to only have sex with people they are dating or have romantic feelings for. You do not need to be in a relationship to have sex with someone, and not all sex only involves two people. Some folks engage in different kinds of sex to affirm their gender identity or sexuality, or to ease anxiety and stress (yes, sex is a great de-stressor!) – the possibilities of sex are endless. People have sex, either solo or with others, for a variety of reasons, in a variety of different ways, with different people, but the *most* important thing is that you're having sex because *you* want to and because you and your partner/s are enjoying it.

It isn't up to us what sex other people like or 'should' engage in – the only sex we need to focus on is the sex we are having with ourselves and others, and how our partner/s feel.

Chapter 8
Beyond Bananas and Condoms

If you read the previous chapter, you know how to have sex, in all its beautiful ways, but now you need to know how to have safer sex and what can happen when things don't go as planned.

Why do I say 'safer sex' rather than 'safe sex'?

This is a phrase I've recently shifted towards and that's because sex is never 100 per cent safe. Even if we do everything the way we should, we dot all the is and cross all the ts, there is still a chance that something may happen, meaning using the term 'safe' just doesn't work. Plus, the implication of 'safe sex' is that there is a way to have perfect sex, meaning when something unplanned happens we feel as if it's our fault or that we should be ashamed. The reality is sometimes things happen that aren't our fault and that's ok. If we know how to have safer sex and react if something does happen that wasn't planned, we will be a-ok! Heck, sex educators themselves have things happen, I've had to use emergency hormonal contraception before, I've had condoms rip inside me, it happens!

The same can be said about sexual health, there is nothing to be ashamed about when it comes to sexual health, and if something does happen or you get an STI, then there are ways to manage it. It's like our general health or mental health, sometimes things happen that are outside of our control. Just as we would visit a doctor if we had a physical injury or concern about our body or mental health, we should visit our doctor or local sexual health clinic if we have concerns about our sexual health. When it comes to sex and sexual health, we should of course try our best to stay safer and look after ourselves, and if something does happen, we need to know what to do from there.

Contraception roulette

The best way to have safer sex is to use contraception and there are plenty to choose from. All individuals, regardless of their gender identity or sexuality and sexual partner/s, should be using contraception. It isn't only to protect against pregnancy. Figuring out what contraception works best for you and the type of sex you're having is vital and that may take some trial and error. As someone who has been on their own contraception during the last three years, I have some words of wisdom: if you aren't happy with a specific contraception and what it's doing to you and your body, change contraception – there's 15 different types, you have options! You are in control of your sexual health, and you get to decide which type you use. So, let's run through your options.

Wrap it up!
Barrier methods are exactly what they say they are – a barrier between yourself and the other individual. Barrier methods

prevent infections being transmitted, as well as protect against pregnancies. Condoms, gloves, finger-cots, dental dams all provide a barrier between yourself and whoever you're being intimate with and can be used by anyone of any gender or any sexuality.

CONDOMS

I *love* them, but it's taken me a few years to truly appreciate them. You may hear people call them 'male condoms' but this isn't inclusive or accurate, so I always use 'external condoms'. External condoms are worn on the penis to prevent semen from entering the vagina or to create a barrier between the penis and whatever it is entering. External condoms can be used by anyone or any gender; whether you have a penis or you're using a strap-on, whether you're penetrating someone's vagina, anus or mouth, condoms are great for all. External condoms are 85 per cent effective when used correctly.

How do you put a condom on a penis or toy?

1. First, you need to check the packaging of the condom to make sure it's in date; you also want to make sure that there is a CE mark or a BSI kite mark, as these symbols indicate that the condom is safe to use. You can find these on the back of individual condoms. If your condom does not have all this information, do not use it.

2. You will also want to check the packaging for any tears or holes; if you notice any holes, bin the condom immediately as it may be ineffective.

3. Now you're ready to open it. Using your thumb, slide the condom to one side of the packet and carefully tear the opposite side. Do not use your teeth or scissors! Then remove the condom from the packet.

4. Now you have the condom outside of the packet, you need to make sure it's the right way up. The best way to do this is to place the condom on the palm of your hand. It should look like a little hat.

5. Place the condom on the tip of the penis or toy, pinch the tip gently and roll the condom down the shaft. If it doesn't roll, that's because it's the wrong way round.

6. When first entering either the anus or vagina, it's important to hold the base of the condom. If the condom rolls up the shaft throughout sex, then it's most likely not the right size. In this case, stop because it isn't safe to have sex with a condom that doesn't truly fit you.

7. After you've finished, hold the base of the condom as you pull out.

8. Remove the condom and dispose of it safely. You will want

to tie a knot in the top of it to stop any semen getting out. Do not flush it down the toilet; wrap it in tissue and throw it in the bin.

External condoms come in a variety of textures – regular, extra-thin, ribbed, extra-ribbed, extra-lube, latex-free – they also come in a variety of sizes and finding your right size is vital. Using the right size condoms not only better protects you, but also makes sex way more enjoyable; if the condom is loose, it may slip off or move around, and if the condom is too tight, it may burst, tear or hurt the individual wearing it. There's no shame in using a small or a medium size condom; all penises of all sizes are perfect the way they are. Using a size that doesn't fit you to impress someone will make sex not as enjoyable and can put you at risk of catching an STI or pregnancy. Figuring out what size condom to use can be fun, and you can ask your partner/s to join in to make it sexy.

Grab yourself a variety of sizes and try them on; obviously you'll need to be erect for this and you won't be able to use the condoms after messing around with them, but honestly the best way to figure out your size is to try them on! You may be thinking, 'I don't have the money to buy five boxes of condoms.' Well, if you're under 25 you can access free condom schemes in the UK, but anyone can pick up free condoms from sexual health clinics, and if you say to them that you're trying to figure out your size, they can give you a variety.

When storing your external condoms, be sure to not put them in a wallet or any place they could be torn or damaged and keep them out of direct sunlight. Some folks buy specific decorated metal boxes that they can keep their condoms in.

INTERNAL CONDOMS

These are 79 per cent effective and are worn inside the vagina to prevent semen from entering the uterus. Internal condoms can also be used for toys too. An internal condom is very similar to an external condom, the only difference is that they have a circular ring inside the latex which helps keep the internal condom in place inside the vagina and they are meant to be looser than external condoms. An internal condom is inserted much like a tampon:

1. Open gently as we spoke about above.
2. Twist the rubber ring at the closed end and insert into the vagina.
3. The rubber ring at the opening must be left outside of the vagina.

Internal condoms were and still are unfortunately referred to as 'female condoms', but again, it isn't only women who use internal condoms. Again, internal condoms must be used properly every time to be effective and should never be used in combination with an external condom.

Condoms get a bad rep in my opinion, but I have come to love using them for sex.* It's crucial to chat with your partner/s about condoms ahead of having sex. Most of the bad rep comes from people not knowing which condoms to use for their body, and

---

* I am a big condom-lover. I think sex education historically has made them 'uncool' when in reality they are *so cool*. Saving time on cleaning up, keeping you safer from STIs and unwanted pregnancies, coming in a variety of textures and flavours – what else could you ask for!

therefore using the wrong size which makes sex not as enjoyable, or not knowing how to put a condom on during sex in a sexy way – some folks get condom shy! Speaking with your partner about what size works for them and how you can incorporate the condom into your sex can make sex better for everyone involved. If the person feels awkward putting the condom on themselves, why not give them a hand? Some folks may also be allergic to certain brands or lubes, so checking in beforehand to ensure that the condoms you're going to use will be ok is important. Some may want to only use vegan brands; in that case, you can stock up on specifically vegan condoms. It's all about finding the right combination for everyone, trial and error, and communication.

DENTAL DAMS

Dental dams are sheets of latex which are placed over the anus or vagina or sex toy for oral sex. Because, guess what, you can get an STI from oral sex! Dental dams come in a variety of colours and flavours. However, these latex sheets are hard to find in stores (they are easier to buy online however), and

> **Myth:** 'Dental dams and external condoms ruin oral sex!' Nope! As I said, dental dams come in a variety of flavours, and so do condoms. If you don't enjoy the taste of latex, then you can grab yourself a fun flavoured one. However, it's important to note that flavoured condoms cannot be used internally for penetration.

when you can find them, they can be expensive compared to other forms of barrier methods. But there is an alternative, you can make your own from the humble condom:

1. First, it's important to do all the same checks you would do if you were using the external condom on a penis or toy.

2. Once you've opened the wrapper, unroll the condom.

3. Cut both ends off the condom and slice up the side to create a flat sheet.

4. Tah-dah! You have yourself a DIY dental dam. Now you can place it over the anus or vagina or toy. You will want to hold this in place with your fingers and even give it a little stretch to cover everything you need to – actual dental dams are *way* stretchier and longer, so if you're struggling with your DIY, it may be worth trying to find actual dental dams.

FINGER-COTS AND GLOVES

These are used solely for penetrating and playing with the vagina, vulva and anus. These are again made of latex and can come with ribs too, for added pleasure. Why do you need to wear finger-cots or gloves for fingering? You may have barely visible cuts on your fingers which can become infected or cause an infection to the other person if you don't wrap it up. It also stops any dirt or germs entering the person's vagina or anus from your nails or fingers.

THE CERVICAL CAP

This is a silicone cap which is shaped to fit snugly around the cervix. These are fitted by a doctor or nurse and are inserted into the vagina and pushed up until it covers the cervix (which is higher than a tampon would go, hence why it must be fitted by a professional). It stays in place because of its suction but it has a little strap to help with the removal. The cup can stay in for up to 46 hours after sex but should stay there for at least six hours. It is 86 per cent effective.

THE DIAPHRAGM

The diaphragm is a shallow cup made of latex which is slightly different to the cervical cap. It is gently pushed into and up the vagina, so it covers the cervix and area around it; they are wider and flatter than the cup, blocking sperm from entering. Like the cup, the diaphragm must be fitted by a nurse or doctor for the first time to find the right fit for the individual and it must be left in the body for at least six hours after sex and no longer than twenty-four hours. You must have a check-up with your doctor once a year to make sure it still fits correctly. The diaphragm and cervical cap are both reusable.

Everyone moans for hormones!

There are also hormonal contraception options. These should be used in collaboration with barrier methods – because they won't protect you from STIs!

THE IMPLANT

The implant is a small rod-like device that is implanted into your arm. This contraception method is used by AFAB individuals. It is 99 per cent effective and lasts up to five years, which is the appeal. It works by increasing your progestin levels which thickens the cervix, stopping sperm from entering the uterus, and may stop eggs from being released.

IUD (INTRAUTERINE DEVICE)

An IUD is a small T-shaped piece of flexible plastic (hormonal) or copper placed into your uterus. The hormonal IUD or coil uses progestin as well and can last up to seven years depending on which brand you use. The copper coil is the sperm's enemy, meaning sperm won't enter the uterus. Both the copper and hormonal coil are 99 per cent effective. However, some folks experience pain when getting an IUD inserted. For a lot of trans folks it simply isn't an option due to body and genital dysphoria, but for trans folks on T who choose to use an IUD, your testosterone will not impact the effectiveness.

THE SHOT
The shot is an injection which again uses progestin. It is 94 per cent effective and needs to be repeated every three months; however, it can take a week to be effective.

THE PILL
The contraceptive pill is 91 per cent effective in practice but this is only if folks don't miss a pill (which reduces its effectiveness). There are a variety of pills, some which you take

Myth: 'The week you bleed on the pill is your period.' Nope! It's actually a 'withdrawal bleed' which may feel and look like you're menstruating but it's just a side effect from taking the break.

every day, some that have a break, some that mean you bleed for a week, some which mean you aren't meant to bleed (but you may still spot/bleed) – finding what pill is right for you is vital, as well as considering the side effects that pill may have.

In 2023, I was part of a Channel 4 documentary called *The Pill Scandal* with Davina McCall and I shared my experience on the pill as a nonbinary individual. I went on the pill as a teenager and, at first, it worked a treat. However, in my early 20s, I started to experience really bad side effects – constant headaches, waking up with extreme nausea, chronic cramping – and my doctor told me to come off it. Coming off the pill meant I had to rely solely on barrier methods, in my case external condoms. In late 2023, I decided to try hormonal birth control again and was placed on a different pill. However, this one didn't agree with me either and I began experiencing side effects that this time made me feel dysphoria – a sore chest for example. So after only a month I came off it. When it comes to the pill it can take three months or so for your body to adjust, but if you really aren't happy with what you're experiencing, you can come off it at any point. At the time of writing this, I am off hormonal birth control and loving using condoms.*

When accessing contraception, trans individuals should feel affirmed and supported in their identity, not deadnamed or misgendered. I was heavily misgendered when I tried the pill again in 2023, even though I had explained to my doctor my gender identity and had even asked if I could take the pill and testosterone at the same time (at the time I was considering whether or not I wanted to transition medically), and she said, and I quote, 'I'm not sure about that trans stuff.' If you don't feel affirmed and heard by your doctor, know that you can ask to see a different person, or even find a trans-friendly doctor or sexual health clinic – though all doctors should respect trans individuals and their sexual health.

THE PATCH

The patch is a fabric square placed on the skin that uses two hormones, progestin and oestrogen. The additional hormones in the patch stop ovulation completely, making it a great option

---

* I could go on and on about the side effects of the pill and I highly recommend you check out Kate Muir's *Everything You Need to Know About the Pill (but were too afraid to ask)* which I feature in!

for trans and gender-diverse+ folks who want to avoid having a period altogether. The patch is 91 per cent effective, though to be truly effective, it needs to be changed on schedule. However, the patch isn't accessible to everyone – those who smoke, or people with migraines with aura, heart conditions, blood pressure issues, blood disorders, diabetes and breast cancer, may not be able to use it. If you are considering the patch, it's important to chat with your doctor beforehand.

THE RING

This is inserted into the vagina once every three weeks. It is made of a flexible material and is inserted in the same way a tampon is, which is why some trans folks find using the ring difficult as it can trigger dysphoria. The ring releases progestin and oestrogen into the body and, after the three weeks, the ring is gently removed, and a withdrawal bleed may occur.

> *What happens if I am on my period whilst the ring is inside me?*
> Nothing! You can use tampons or a menstrual cup whilst also using the ring, but be sure to not accidentally pull the ring out when you remove your tampon or cup.

Sterilization

Sterilization is a permanent contraception that folks may choose later in life or if they never want to have children. There are surgical procedures that folks can undergo which stop the sperm from entering your ejaculate or stop eggs from reaching the uterus. However, the body can heal itself in a way that means some of these procedures may not be 100 per cent effective forever, which is why using contraception at the same time is important.

Multi-tasking contraception

It's important to use contraception that protects from both STIs and pregnancies, and that may mean multi-tasking, using two forms of contraception at once. Even if you're on the pill, you'll still need to use a barrier method.

Emergency contraception

As I said at the beginning of this chapter, I've had to use emergency contraception before, and though it was scary at the time, I know now I only felt that way as no one had spoken to me about emergency contraception before. So, I hope I can ease some of those anxieties or fears you may experience. Emergency contraception is used after unprotected sex to prevent a pregnancy from occurring. Whether your contraception failed you, or something happened that wasn't planned, or you didn't use it and you don't want to be pregnant, you have options on what to do next.

The most effective emergency contraception method is getting an IUD fitted. An IUD is great as a regular form of contraception, but it is also a great emergency contraception. It can be used up to five days after unprotected sex or up to five days after the earliest day you could have ovulated. Once the IUD is fitted you will have protection from an unexpected pregnancy for years until you have it removed, making it a great long-term option for folks who don't want to have children any time soon. And even though getting the IUD fitted may trigger trans and gender-diverse+ folks' dysphoria, once it's in you can forget about it.

If getting an IUD isn't for you, then there is the option of an emergency contraception pill, also known as 'the morning-after pill'. There are two options for the emergency contraception pill, Levonelle and ellaOne. These must be taken within three to five days after the unprotected sex. However, emergency pills won't work if you're already ovulating as they work by delaying your ovulation, and several studies show that most morning-after pills won't work if an individual is over 195 pounds (though sadly, most folks aren't told this when they purchase the pill).

If you're a trans man or someone who is taking testosterone, you can take the morning-after pill or get an IUD, but if you have concerns, do chat with the pharmacist or your doctor.

As I said, I've taken ellaOne and it worked for me; unfortunately as a trans person, accessing the morning-after pill can be tricky because it means 'outing' yourself to the doctor or pharmacist or dealing with gendered phrases that don't reflect everyone who may need access to it. If you're a trans individual and you need to access the emergency pill, you can ask to speak to the pharmacist or someone at the sexual health clinic privately. It's important that you know that you deserve access to contraception and emergency contraception whilst also having your gender identity affirmed and respected.

Let's talk about abortion

Throughout this book I really want to make sure I use the correct language when referring to difficult or uncomfortable conversations, and 'abortion' is one of those words I think many people are afraid to use or are uncomfortable using.

If you become pregnant and don't want to be, or can't be, then you may choose to have an abortion and that is a decision made totally by you and one that should be respected. Abortion is a common medical procedure to end a pregnancy and, in the UK, one in three cis women and folks who can fall pregnant will have an abortion by the time they are 45.* Anyone can have an abortion, not only cis women, but anyone with the capacity to become pregnant can get an abortion. Abortion is a simpler procedure the earlier into the pregnancy an individual is, so if you believe you may be pregnant it's important to take a pregnancy test as soon as possible.

Why may someone have an abortion? There are countless reasons why someone may choose to have an abortion, and regardless of the reason, their decision should be respected. Having an abortion is a medical procedure, one that is safe, and much like any other procedure it doesn't have to be a 'big thing'. Some folks may be emotional about having an abortion, some may have no feelings towards having one; you are valid in your feelings and your decision.

There are two types of abortion – medical and surgical – both are legal, safe and effective, but choosing the right one for you is a conversation you will have with a healthcare professional and is based on where you are in the pregnancy.

Medical abortion

A medical abortion involves taking two medications, mifepristone to end the pregnancy, and misoprostol which causes the womb to contract so the pregnancy leaves the body. This can feel like a very heavy period. This type of abortion is the most effective and safe option for those who are up to ten weeks into a pregnancy; however, under supervision, it can be taken up to 24 weeks into a pregnancy.

---

* www.gov.uk/government/statistics/abortion-statistics-for-england-and-wales-2021/abortion-statistics-england-and-wales-2021

Surgical abortion

A surgical abortion physically removes the pregnancy in one of two ways: vacuum aspiration, which removes the pregnancy through suction, or dilation and evacuation, which removes the pregnancy using forceps. Vacuum aspiration is used up to 15 weeks into a pregnancy, whilst a dilation and evacuation is used after 15 weeks.

You can choose to have an abortion up until 24 weeks into a pregnancy, but beyond that there has to be a medical reason for it. If your life is in danger, or the foetus has severe foetal abnormalities, you can have an abortion later in your pregnancy, though this rarely happens.

But where do I go if I need an abortion? You can refer yourself directly by contacting an abortion provider, or you can ask your doctor or sexual health clinic to refer you.

When abortion isn't an option

Some folks may not wish to go ahead with an abortion, for whatever reason, and that's totally valid. Another option for those who do not want to have a child but do not want to go ahead with an abortion is adoption.

STIs aren't scary

We've spoken about how to best protect ourselves and what to do if we or our partner falls pregnant, but pregnancy isn't the only thing that can occur if we have unprotected sex, or something doesn't go to plan. Anyone of any gender or sexuality can get a sexually transmitted infection (STI), and they are super common.

Most folks will have an STI at least once in their lifetime, yet we treat STIs as this super scary thing when, in reality, it happens. The fear of STIS comes from society's views on them, but having an STI means nothing about you as an individual, or who you're having sex with, or your sex life, or how 'clean' you are. Even us sex educators will get an STI because, as I've said, there is *no perfect sex*. You can get an STI at any stage of your life, even if you're using barrier methods correctly, regardless of how many partners you have – sometimes it just happens. Sadly, even though one million new infections happen every single day, most of us battle the stigma and shame that surrounds STIs and getting tested, but let's unlearn that together right now!

The alphabet soup of STIs

There are 30 viruses, bacterial infections and parasites that we know of that you can get from having sex – please don't let that put you off from having sex, instead use it as a reminder of why trying to have safer sex is vital but also that getting an STI is totally common.

C is for Chlamydia

Chlamydia is the most common STI in the UK, making up half of the recorded STI infections and, guess what, it's totally treatable with simple antibiotics. There's one catch though, 75 per cent of folks with a vagina and 50 per cent of folks with a penis have zero signs of the infection, which is why I said 'recorded' infections as many go unrecorded... meaning there is likely far more folks with it. If it is left untreated, it can make it harder to fall pregnant later in life.

What are the symptoms *if* you have them?

◎ Pain when you pee
◎ Discharge from your vagina, penis or anus that isn't 'normal' to you (which is why understanding what your 'normal' is is vital)
◎ Painful and/or swollen testicles
◎ Bleeding between periods or during or after sex
◎ For folks with a vagina, pain in the stomach during sex.

G is for Gonorrhoea (a dyslexic's worst nightmare!)

Gonorrhoea is like chlamydia's twin, not identical but nearly. It's another often symptomless STI but, again, totally common, and treatable – but it has its own nickname, 'the clap'. Half of vagina owners have no symptoms, whilst 10 per cent of penis owners don't. If left untreated, gonorrhoea can cause serious health complications.

Symptoms include:

◎ Pain in your stomach
◎ A thick green or yellow discharge from the vagina or penis
◎ A burning sensation when you pee
◎ Bleeding between periods (which is why tracking your periods is important!)
◎ Conjunctivitis (if your eyes are infected; yup STIS don't only affect your genitals)
◎ Pain or unusual discharge from your anus.

G is for Genital warts

Genital warts fall into the same group as HPV. You can get warts

BEYOND BANANAS AND CONDOMS

in the entrance or inside the vagina, around the cervix, anywhere on the penis, scrotum or urethra, in or around the anus or on your upper thighs. Unfortunately, even if you use barrier methods, you can still get genital warts and HPV viruses because they can simply be passed on by skin-on-skin contact.

Treatment varies on the size and location of the warts but typically includes the use of a cream or lotion, or removal with heat or through freezing.

H is for Hepatitis B, Herpes, HIV (that's a lot of Hs!)

Hepatitis B affects the liver and is the leading cause of liver cancer. Hepatitis B is passed on through sexual intercourse or blood to blood contact and, in 2022, it was recorded that 0.3 per cent of the UK population have chronic hepatitis B.

Symptoms include:

- Pain or bloating
- Fatigue
- Dark urine and pale or clay-coloured stool
- Low grade fever, nausea, vomiting
- Itching
- Loss of appetite.

The herpes simplex virus (HSV) has two types – HSV1 and HSV2 – it is again super common but often undiagnosed because most folks don't even realize they have it. Herpes can be found in the mouth or nose (often causing a cold) and genitals and can be con-tracted through sex and kissing during or just after an outbreak. I don't want to scare you, but once you have herpes, the virus, you have it for life – and there's no cure; however, it can be managed to keep outbreaks under control. Your first outbreak will be the worst, but like most colds or flus, once you've had it once, it gets easier to manage. If you are having an outbreak, it's important to not kiss or be intimate with anyone during or just after said outbreak. You're more likely to have an outbreak if you're ill, or stressed, or smoking or drinking too much alcohol, or wearing underwear that isn't cotton.

Symptoms include:

◉ Pain, discomfort and itching when peeing
◉ Unusual discharge
◉ Fluid-filled blisters that turn into sores
◉ Cold, snotty and runny nose.

HIV stands for 'human immunodeficiency virus'; it attacks the immune system. In the 1980s, being diagnosed with HIV was considered a death sentence, and, sadly, in many areas of the world today, it still is. HIV hit the gay community the hardest and became known as a 'gay disease', but anyone can be diagnosed with HIV, anyone of any gender, sexuality, race or age. If HIV is unmanaged, it can go on to cause AIDS, acquired immune deficiency syndrome, which is the most advanced stage of the HIV infection. Someone with AIDS will find it hard to fight off infections and diseases that those without AIDS can easily recover from. You cannot catch AIDS, but you can contract HIV, which can become AIDS if untreated.

HIV is passed on through the exchange of bodily fluids, semen and blood. HIV is *not* contracted through kissing, or from sitting on a toilet seat. It can be passed on through unprotected sex, or sharing sex toys, or sharing needles to inject drugs, or through contaminated blood. Someone who is HIV positive can pass on HIV to their child when giving birth, although this is very rare in the UK.

Early symptoms of HIV can include:

- ◉ Flu-like symptoms
- ◉ Headaches
- ◉ Sore throat, swollen lymph nodes, nausea
- ◉ Fever.

So how do we protect ourselves from catching HIV?

- ◉ Safer sex practices, using barrier methods such as condoms, finger-cots, dental dams etc
- ◉ Taking precautions to avoid bodily fluids being exchanged
- ◉ Knowing your status, which means getting tested (more on that shortly)
- ◉ Taking PrEP (pre-exposure prophylaxis) if we are going to engage in sex. PrEP can protect you against HIV even if you don't wear a condom, though it doesn't protect you from other STIs. PrEP is most used by the queer community, primarily by AMAB individuals who have sex with other AMAB individuals
- ◉ Taking PEP (post-exposure prophylaxis) if we are fearful that we have been exposed. This can be taken up to three days after the exposure, though it works best when taken within twenty-four hours. Though it does reduce the risk of contracting HIV after you've been exposed, it isn't a guarantee.

In the UK, treatment for HIV has come a long way and it isn't something to be feared or ashamed of. HIV treatment is now very effective, meaning HIV positive folks can live a long and healthy life just by taking a pill every day to keep the amount of the virus in their blood undetectable.

U=U
Undetectable means untransmittable – folks whose virus levels are undetectable are unable to transmit the virus to someone else, meaning they can have a full and healthy sex life without the worry of passing on the virus even when having unprotected sex.

P is for Parasites
Parasitic STIs are caused by teeny tiny bugs... yes, bugs, and there are a few different types. You may feel itchy, you may squirm, cross and uncross your legs but you won't be itching forever. There are ways to get rid of them and, luckily, most are harmless.

P IS ALSO FOR PUBIC LICE
You may know pubic lice by the more commonly used name 'crabs'. Why? Because they look like tiny little crabs when you put them under a microscope of course! These can be found in the pubic areas but also in other areas too where there is coarse hair, such as your legs and underarms. And just like lice on your head, they can hop from one person to another. How do you spot them if they are so teeny tiny? You will feel very itchy, but you may also see tiny lice eggs attached to the hair, as well as small specks of blood and black powder on your skin, underwear or sheets. Pubic lice can be treated though but must be diagnosed by your doctor first and provided with special treatment. Removing the hair may

be a short-term solution, but treatment is necessary to make sure they don't come back.

S IS FOR SCABIES

Scabies spread by skin-to-skin contact or shared fabrics – beds, couches, towels – but these don't live in the hair, they make themselves a home under the skin. Scabies cause itching, especially after a hot shower or bath or at night, as well as red rashes and silver tracks on the skin where the scabies have burrowed under the skin. These rashes can appear anywhere but are typically seen between the fingers and toes, wrists, elbows, stomach, buttocks, genitals of men and AMAB folks and the nipples of women and AFAB folks. These too can be treated with insecticide from the pharmacy.

Myth: Blue waffle is real! If you're like me, you grew up with the urban myth of 'blue waffle'. It was a viral image that went around in 2010 but is still brought up in classroom conversation across the world today. The image (which I highly recommend you *don't* google) featured a vulva which looked irritated and infected, possibly even injured. I remember seeing this image and being terrified of vulvas, including my own which I hadn't investigated yet. The reality is no one knows what was happening in the photo, if the person knew their photo had been shared, or whether the individual had an STI or not, but 'blue waffle' was born. But it's simply a myth, it isn't real. The 'blue waffle' cannot hurt you.

S is for Syphilis

Syphilis is contracted through unprotected sex or skin-on-skin contact and can present itself on the penis, anus, rectum, vagina, tongue or lips. If left untreated, syphilis can infect other parts of the body such as the brain, nerves, eyes, heart, bones, skin or blood vessels and can lead to death – though this happened a lot in the past, unfortunately to sex workers, this is way less common now, with most folks making a full recovery with the help of antibiotics.

Symptoms include:

- Sores which are often painless appearing where the infection happened
- Swelling of lymph glands
- Non-itchy skin rash
- Fatigue
- Headaches and eye pain or vision issues.

Trying to get pregnant

Sexual health isn't only important when trying not to catch an STI or fall pregnant, it's also just as important if you do want to have children!

It may seem like getting pregnant is easy – sadly sex ed of the past really tried to convince people that even looking at someone you find sexually attractive could 'knock you up' – but it really isn't that easy, and some folks struggle to conceive.

Fertility

As someone who doesn't want to be pregnant, understanding my cycle, how I could fall pregnant and my fertility is crucial – and the same goes for someone who wants to conceive. Our fertility can change over time, which is why understanding our fertility from an earlier age can be beneficial if we want to start a family in the future. In the UK, one in seven heterosexual and cisgender couples have fertility issues, but infertility can affect anyone for a variety of reasons.* Fertility issues do not necessarily mean you can't ever conceive, it may just take a little longer or require some medical help along the way.

Sex is fun, but safer sex is where it's at.

---

* www.nhs.uk/conditions/infertility

Chapter 9
Beyond Boyfriend and Girlfriend

Relationships come in all shapes and sizes, all different lengths and commitments, varying in number of people involved.

For most of us, society presents relationships as being a romantic bond between two people, typically a man and a woman, but this isn't always the case. We have already learnt about the different forms of attraction, romantic and sexual, and those attraction types will lead to different relationship dynamics, which will involve varying levels of intimacy and maybe even varying numbers of people.

Different types of relationship dynamics

Monogamous
A monogamous relationship is a relationship with only one partner at a time.

Non-monogamous
Non-monogamy is a term used to describe any relationship that

doesn't involve only two people, and there's a few different types of non-monogamous relationship dynamics:

- ◉ **Open relationships:** These are when a couple agree that they are both free to be intimate with other people. Typically, it's only sex, and romantic relationships with other people are not ok.

> **Myth:** 'Only men and bisexuals want open relationships because they are greedy.' *Nope.* Folks of all gender identities and sexualities engage in non-monogamous and open relationships and it has *zero* to do with being greedy (unless you want to identify as greedy then *go for it!*). It's simply about wanting to be intimate or in a relationship with more than one person, and if everyone is on board and there is open communication, the more the merrier.

- ◉ **Poly:** Literally meaning 'many loves', being poly means to love or have a romantic relationship with more than one person.
- ◉ **Hierarchical polyamory:** This is where an individual will have a main partner (or a nest partner) alongside other relationships.
- ◉ **Egalitarian polyamory:** This is where every partner is considered equal. These folks may all live together in a triad and quad.
- ◉ **Solo polyamory:** Referring to one person who engages with others who have other partners.
- ◉ **Relationship anarchists:** Referring to people who question distinctions between friends and partners and may have many close people in their lives.

T4T

Trans Loving Trans or Trans for Trans is a term that refers to a trans individual who is actively dating or seeking out other trans folks to date. This includes all non-cisgender folks – nonbinary, genderfluid, gender-diverse+ folks.

Why do some trans folks only date/only want to date other trans folks?

- There is a greater understanding of how one another feels or navigates spaces as trans individuals.
- There isn't a need to educate the other person on general trans topics or terms etc.
- There is an element of added safety when in a relationship with another trans person.
- Trans people are just cool!

As I'm writing this, I am in my first T4T relationship with a trans man and it has been an extremely fulfilling and euphoric experience, for all of the reasons above.

Situationships

A situationship is a romantic relationship that hasn't been explicitly defined, leaving it in this strange grey area. The relationship may have many of the same qualities as an official relationship, but the people involved have simply not put labels on it. This is usually intentional, whether that's to avoid making things too complicated, or because they're still figuring out what they want from each other. You don't necessarily need to label your relationship if everyone involved understands the boundaries of said situationship.

Casual sex can fall under 'situationships'. Some people don't want any kind of relationship and are purely looking for sex, intimacy and that's it. This type of relationship may also be called

'friends with benefits', 'sex bud-
dies' or 'sneaky links'. It's really
important that you are clear
about your intentions when
starting something casual with
someone new, and that you
make sure you communicate
with each other.

Queerplatonic

Queerplatonic, also called
qplatonic relationships, is a
term for an intimate, non-
romantic committed relationship. This relationship typically
goes beyond what is considered normal or socially acceptable
for a platonic relationship but is not romantic in nature or does
not fully fit the traditional idea of a romantic relationship. These
relationships may look like friendships, or situationships, or even
romantic relationships, involving different levels of intimacy
(even sex).

Plus not minus

Regardless of what type of relationship you're in, a relationship
should always add something to your life, not take anything away.
Regardless of your gender identity or sexuality or relationship dy-
namic, you can find yourself in unhealthy and toxic relationships,
or even you could be the unhealthy one.*

> **Myth:** 'Sex is the most
> important thing in a relation-
> ship.' *Nope!* Some folks have
> healthy, fulfilling relation-
> ships without engaging in sex
> ever! When Brook, the sexual
> health organization, asked
> folks what the most impor-
> tant thing in a relationship is,
> sex didn't make the top ten!
> Rather laughing, sharing val-
> ues and feeling supported and
> secure were the most impor-
> tant thing to young people.

---

* I am the first person to hold my hand up and say I haven't been the
healthiest person in some of my previous relationships. Whether it's down
to previous trauma seeping back in, or generally just being the bad guy, I've

Healthy relationships should always add value, so what should we be looking for in a relationship, the good, the bad, the pink?

Greenflags, redflags, pinkflags?

Greenflags

These are good signs that appear when first dating someone or when in a relationship with someone. These are signs that the person you're dating or in a relationship with is healthy or is working on becoming healthier (as we all should be doing) and aligns with your needs and desires. Your greenflags will look different from mine; greenflags are completely down to personal preference and lived experience, but what they boil down to is how you feel about this person and/or the relationship.** Sometimes greenflags come out of nowhere, perhaps someone you're dating doesn't necessarily tick your pre-made list of greenflags but creates new ones, which is super exciting.

General greenflags you may look out for:

- Supporting your work, future, goals and actively asking you about these topics
- Respect, loyalty and communication
- Similar morals or views on the world, politics etc
- Feeling safe around them
- Not feeling intimidated by them, or their friends and family
- Enjoying your time together and generally having fun
- Having similar interests and hobbies

been there. But knowing that has made me a better partner now because I check in with myself if I feel any of these unhealthy behaviours arise.
** Greenflags also don't need to be huge, they can be the little things, sometimes the bare minimum if you're someone like me who has experienced abuse.

- ⊙ Understanding each other's boundaries
- ⊙ Validating each other's identities.

But these are just general ones, your own personal list of green-flags may be more... unique shall we say. Here's mine for example:

DEE'S GREENFLAG LIST

- ⊙ Uses my correct pronoun, name and language that is gender-affirming
- ⊙ Engages in politics
- ⊙ Likes and reshares my posts
- ⊙ Hypes me and my work up, showing me off to their friends and family
- ⊙ Offers to split the bill rather than pay for it in full
- ⊙ Likes rats.

Redflags

Redflags are the opposite of green ones – they are signs that tell you to *run*. These are signs that the person is toxic, unhealthy or even dangerous and that you should leave the relationship immediately.

General redflags include:

- ⊙ Signs of aggression, violence or an inability to control temper
- ⊙ Lying or dishonesty
- ⊙ No clear boundaries or oversteps and ignores your boundaries
- ⊙ Reliance on you with no other support system

- Jealousy or possessiveness*
- Making you feel like everything is your fault and that you're hard to love.

CONTROLLING BEHAVIOUR

Controlling behaviour is another redflag, but it's one I wanted to dedicate some time to exploring. Your partner/s should never control you or your life; of course, they can help you by giving suggestions or advice, but you should always have the final say. If your partner is controlling you, this is abuse.

There are a few ways abuse can appear in a relationship:

- **Sexual:** someone forcing you to engage in sexual acts, touching you without your consent, withdrawing or sabotaging contraception, filming or taking photos of you without your consent.
- **Physical:** someone hitting, throwing things or hurting you. Even if the person doesn't actually do these things but threatens to, this is still abusive.**

---

* The green-eyed monster – jealousy. It is 100% normal (whatever that means) to feel jealous or envious in a relationship because it's a totally natural feeling. Jealousy, however, can become sour if you are resulting in unhealthy ways to channel feelings of jealousy such as saying nasty comments, or controlling your partner etc. You can work through feelings of jealousy by simply communicating with your partner, and if these feelings do not subside or if they become unhealthy, then yes – it may be a redflag.

** I want to talk here briefly about the 'Kyle' trope or 'joke'. You may have heard of it, but if you haven't, it refers to a made-up person (typically a cisgender boy) called Kyle who punches holes in walls when he is angry. This isn't a joke – it is abusive. If someone is breaking things in your home, or punching walls, it isn't just a funny 'Kyle' moment. We need to call it what it is – abuse.

- ◎ **Verbal:** someone insulting, humiliating, swearing or making threats at/towards you.
- ◎ **Emotional:** someone ignoring your needs and feelings, gaslighting you, making you question your own memories or threatening to leave the relationship.*
- ◎ **Financial:** someone controlling what you can spend your money on, giving you a budget, stopping you from working, or taking your money from you.

POWER IMBALANCE

A power imbalance is when one person in a relationship has more power than the other person, and this can take many forms:

- ◎ **Age differences:** if one partner is older/younger than the other.
- ◎ **Financial:** if one person earns more money than the other.
- ◎ **Authority:** if one person has more authority than the other that's given to them through their job. The people in the relationship might work together or one of them may have a job that gives them more power over the other outside of work, for example celebrities, civil servants.

---

* I've spoken very openly online about the emotional abuse I experienced which resulted in various therapy trips and medication for anxiety. You may see phrases like 'gaslighting' being thrown around when discussing emotional abuse and it can feel almost like a buzz word now – but the reality is, gaslighting is utterly devastating, and as someone who is still in recovery from it, it's truly damaging. Gaslighting is when someone (in my case a previous partner) makes you question your own perception of reality to control you. Even to do this I am unsure of what moments were real and what moments were fabricated by him.

Now if you are finding yourself saying 'oh that's me!' – do not fear. These power imbalances aren't always something to be concerned about; however, sometimes it can be problematic and lead to abuse.

Some signs that an imbalance is problematic are:

- ⊙ Feeling that you have less experience than your partner
- ⊙ Being reliant on your partner for certain things
- ⊙ Feeling that your partner knows best about relationships and sex because they have more experience
- ⊙ Feeling the need to 'prove' your maturity to them
- ⊙ Feeling like you can't speak your mind because they have the ability to affect your job/career
- ⊙ Modifying your behaviour because of them
- ⊙ Feeling that you don't have control over the relationship
- ⊙ Feeling uncomfortable telling family or friends because they 'won't understand'
- ⊙ Being asked to do things that you're uncomfortable with.

WHAT I LIKE TO CALL THE 'GIDEON GRAVES THEORY'

We started this book talking about my gay awakening – Ramona Flowers – and now we return to her again. This is a theory I coined after watching *Scott Pilgrim vs the World* for the thousandth time. To summarize, before dating Scott, Ramona dated someone called Gideon Graves (the villain of the movie), and after she and Scott break up, she goes back to him. When Scott says 'Like, hello, he was horrid to you, why are you going back?, she says, 'He has a way of getting into my head.' In Ramona's case, she has a chip in her head that literally means Gideon can enter her head when he wants – but it's a metaphor for toxic, controlling individuals in relationships and how victims feel. We may not have a chip in our head, but it can feel like it sometimes. It's also why some folks may stay in abusive situations.

WE HAVE TO TALK ABOUT CHEATING

What counts as cheating varies from person to person, relationship to relationship, so it's important to understand your own feelings about cheating as well as your partner/s to build a secure framework for your unique relationship and to outline 'rules'. Sometimes, people can break rules unknowingly because they have different ideas from their partner/s about what counts as cheating. Other times, people know they have broken the rules.

But why do people cheat? There's many different reasons as to why people cheat, but here's a few general reasons:

- Feeling bored in their relationship or with their partner.
- Wanting to end the relationship but being unsure how to.
- Feeling insecure and wanting attention, from their partner and/or from someone else.
- Not thinking about the consequences and getting lost in the moment.
- Wanting to cheat and not caring about the consequences.
- Finding it exciting to take risks.

WHAT TO DO IF YOU THINK YOUR PARTNER HAS CHEATED

Most of us have been there. Worrying and feeling anxious if you think your partner has cheated on you, but if you focus on healthy and calm communication, a better outcome is likely. Unless you have evidence that someone is cheating on you, it's important to be careful of accusing them outright. If you're wrong, it could damage your relationship and hurt the other person. Instead, stay calm, raise the concern to your partner, listen and take a moment to react.

And to those who have cheated on their partner, it's important to ask yourself why you have cheated. Knowing the 'why' helps you to figure out your next steps, i.e. whether you should tell your partner or not, whether you should end the relationship or not, if things can be fixed. It's a difficult position to be in and the situation is never a nice one, but it's important to take responsibility and to feel your feelings – which may be shame, rage, embarrassment, anxiety or excitement and joy (if you are happy about this, you must consider how your partner would feel and why you feel joy over this).

LET'S ANSWER SOME QUESTIONS ON REDFLAGS

'Is it normal to argue in a relationship or is this a redflag?

Arguing in a relationship is 100 per cent normal. Disagreeing as a couple isn't a bad thing, it just shows that you are both individuals and may have different outlooks on the same thing. However, if you are constantly arguing, and these arguments are becoming more serious or upsetting, or if the other person is always 'picking a fight', purposely trying to argue with you about only small things, then this may be a redflag.

Are white lies redflags?

Lying and dishonesty is a redflag, but most of us tell little white lies every now and then such as 'No, I love that T-shirt

BEYOND BANANAS AND CONDOMS

that says "big mummy milkers" on it'. However, if someone is lying to you about important things, then yes, this is a redflag.

Pinkflags

Pinkflags are subtle signs that you might not be a fit in a relationship. These are also signs you may talk yourself out of or overlook in the early stages of a relationship until they become redflags and deal breakers for the relationship.

General pinkflags may look like:

- Political or religious differences
- Different moral beliefs such as eating meat or drinking alcohol
- Unmatched love languages
- Unmatched energy in texting, or intimacy.

Boundaries

I'm not going to lie, I have mastered setting boundaries for myself in relationships. It isn't only romantic relationships that you should set boundaries in; all forms of relationships need boundaries, and you can set boundaries around all sorts of things including money, sex, health, touch etc.

How do you set a boundary?

1. Decide on the boundary that you're wanting to set, e.g. not wanting anyone to touch your belly button (yes, this is about me).

2. Tell those who need to know this boundary, i.e. anyone who may touch you, such as your tattooist, your partner, doctors etc.

3. Be consistent in reminding these people of your boundary, e.g. 'Hey, remember I don't like my belly button being touched.'

It's ok if it is them

Break-ups suck and they aren't always simple, but they are part of the circle of relationships.

But the whole 'it isn't you, it's me'... we need to ditch this because most of the time it is the other person – and that's ok! Sometimes you just don't gel as much as you thought you might, your pinkflags may just be too important to ignore or maybe there just isn't a reason and you just want to break up; simply not wanting to be with someone is always enough.

Possible reasons for breaking up with someone:

◉ You aren't happy in the relationship. The relationship doesn't spark joy any more.
◉ Your future goals don't align.
◉ You constantly disagree and cannot seem to resolve your problems.
◉ The idea of staying with your current partner feels overwhelming.
◉ You fantasize about breaking up.
◉ You find yourself distancing yourself from your partner.
◉ You don't feel safe in the relationship.

Ending it sucks

Ending relationships is not easy and there isn't a 'right' way to do it – it's totally down to you how you end a relationship. I've been dumped, I've been the dumper, I've been dumped over text, in person in a park, and via a friend of a friend. So, here are my tips for being the dumper and the dumpee!

Dumper tips

- Consider how you would like to be broken up with.
- Respect your ex during the break-up; avoid being mean or bringing up past drama unless it's relevant to the breaking up.
- If you want to do it via text (or have to if you're long distance), write the text out in your notes app first and read over it before pressing send. You could also get a close friend you trust to read it too.
- If you want to do it via video call or voice call, prepare what you're going to say beforehand.
- You don't owe your ex a beautifully written, three-page Shakespearean explanation of why you are breaking up, but giving some clarity is important.
- Be clear about where you both stand now and what the future will look like – will you go no-contact, will you meet up to exchange hoodies etc?
- If you feel unsafe and you want the break-up to be quick, followed by blocking or ghosting, that is ok.

Dumpee tips

- Allow yourself to feel. You don't have to be a stone-cold killer when being broken up with, you're allowed to be emotional and cry.
- You don't have to respond right away – you can take a moment, or even a day, to respond.
- If you have any questions, feel free to ask your ex, but it may be best to ask these once you've calmed down.
- Don't be mean towards your ex; the relationship has ended but that isn't the end of the world, and they aren't the villain in the situation.

It doesn't matter what kind of relationship you're in, and with whom – if you're happy, it's consensual and legal then it's all gravy! And if you don't want anything romantic, that's also ok!

Chapter 10
Beyond Nudes and Emojis

I spent most of my teen and young adult years online and I was *not* trying to be safe online. It's only in adulthood that I've really learnt how to be safe online.

Again, this is another chapter where I will put a content warning as we will be covering topics surrounding sexual assault and sexual image-based abuse.

Before we get into online safety, I want to start by saying that the internet can be a scary or difficult place to navigate, but it can also be wonderful. I hope I've made it clear throughout that I am a believer in giving folks the tools to navigate difficult or possibly unsafe situations rather than telling them 'don't go there' or 'don't do that', because, guess what, people will still go there and do the thing you told them not to do. The internet itself isn't evil or bad, it's simply a space where all the rubbish and stereotypes from society is projected for all to see, where people who we may not necessarily interact with in person can send us messages, and where content we would stay away from seeps into our feed. People tend to think they are safe to share their controversial opinions or mean beliefs online because they are behind a screen, but those people have these thoughts in real life too. Social media shines a light on the good, the bad, the ugly that is already in the world, now just at your fingertips, which is why if you know how to navigate it safely, you'll be fine! Ultimately, risk is a normal part of navigating online spaces, but once we know how to safely navigate the possible risks, the internet isn't such a bad place.

Digital footprint

A digital footprint is a trail of information about yourself that you leave when you use the internet. These 'footprints' are used by businesses to send you targeted apps based on your online searching and history. It's also what people may see if they do a little googling, like your future employer or partner, which is why it's important to think before you post. It's also another reason why a 2023 survey found that more than half of LGBTQIA+ users are leaving social media due to safety concerns relating to their digital footprint.*

I'm an oversharer, you're an oversharer!
'Hi, I'm Dee and I'm an oversharer.'

I have worked hard on establishing boundaries with what I post and share online, because previously I was sharing *way* too much and it eventually made me feel really uncomfortable.** I think most young people share their life online as they want to

---

* https://glaad.org/publications/social-media-safety-index-2023
** I say this but in 2023 I found out that one of my younger brothers followed my work page, meaning there is a high chance he saw my post on giving head to a vulva owner for the first time... so yeah, don't be me.

find others like them, their own community, and that's certainly why I started to share my gender journey online. But also, most people share stuff online because they want their friends and family (and sometimes following) to know how they are, to celebrate their wins, and to show off the people in their life. It's imperative to share what you feel comfortable with sharing, and this may change throughout your life. As a teen and young adult, I wanted to share every part of my life online, but as I've moved into adulthood, I'm more aware of the content I am sharing with the world and my following, and realized I didn't want people to know everything about my life. Now I think before I post and post only what I want to post.

Someone I used to know was very offline, only posting every now and then, keeping most of his life to himself, and this was strange at first to me as I was so used to sharing everything online. But I think he showed me that you don't need to post 24/7 and that you can keep some things, especially relationship things, to yourself.

But it's also important to know that what people do share online is typically the highlights, or what they want people to see, especially when it comes to relationships.

You + internet = ???
As I've already said, I've set boundaries with my social media intake – 'we are on a break', so to speak. It's important to know how the internet makes us feel so that, depending on those feelings, we can set boundaries on how much time we spend on social media, or how much we share online, or whether we even want to share anything personal online (keep this in mind, we will come back to it!). If doom scrolling on TikTok makes you feel bad about

yourself, your body, your life, then it could be time to break up with your social media, or at least take a break.

Sometimes it isn't about how much time you're spending on social media, it's also about what kind of content you're engaging with, what profiles you're following, what articles and videos you're consuming. Your feed should make you happy and that will look different for each individual person. For me, my feed looks like LGBTQIA+ people, *Five Nights at Freddy's* theories and fan costumes, horror-fandoms, educational content and more (really exposing myself here). Those are things that make me happy (or feed into my special interests) and your feed should make you feel good too – it should spark joy and make you feel euphoric. If your feed doesn't do that then maybe it's time to unfollow some people or try searching for things that do spark joy.

On the topic of unfollowing people, it is always your right to unfollow a person or a page which doesn't make you feel good. That includes friends or people you know within an online space. It's also ok to mute certain words or phrases or names of people – I'm looking at you, J.K. Rowling – to make your online space a better place for you. Particularly for LGBTQIA+ people, protecting our wellbeing is vital, and if that means blocking specific words or phrases that may harm us then that's completely valid! You can also block people, which can stop them from ever interacting with you or your content again. When it comes to messages, you don't need to open or reply to any message you receive. As a trans content creator, I receive a lot of messages from folks and sometimes those messages aren't kind. So, I simply ignore them, or delete them, report them, or block the account, and that is totally valid.

Earlier this year, I realized how much social media was impacting me. I realized I was obsessed with consuming trans content, spending hours of my day staring at other people's transition and coming-out videos, and get-ready with mes, and at the same time, I started feeling worse about myself. But I didn't link the two together. I felt incredibly unhappy with where I was in my transition and looked at others thinking 'god I wish I looked like that' or 'I can't wait to go through that', whilst also looking at myself and thinking 'I am not enough'. Then one day it clicked, those videos were the reason I was feeling so dysphoric, and that's when I started to set boundaries for what content I consumed and how often I consumed it. Trust me, it was difficult to do that because social media is designed to be addictive and it is easy to spend hours on your phone in a blink of an eye or follow people you'd like to take inspiration from who actually make you feel bad about yourself, but once you start, it becomes second nature.

So, what's your relationship with social media like? Once you know that, you can moderate it.

LGBTQIA+ web-surfing!

For many LGBTQIA+ individuals, online spaces are the only spaces they can express themselves or exist openly; they are where they find others like themselves, or learn more about their identities, or date people. But the internet can also be a really harmful place for LGBTQIA+ folks.

Privacy settings

As we have already discussed, only you get to define your boundaries, and this goes for online too. You can do this via your privacy settings. This includes choosing who gets to see or interact with your profile. Some LGBTQIA+ people may choose to have a private personal account as they want to be online but aren't ready to be out in person. It can be a great way to find community and to slowly explore being out whilst safely having control over who knows your identity. Choosing to be private on social media for many LGBTQIA+ folks is a way of being able to

> **Myth:** 'It's dangerous to be LGBTQIA+ online.' Not necessarily. Nine in ten LGBTQIA+ young people (90 per cent) say they can be themselves online, and nearly all LGBTQIA+ young people (95 per cent) say the internet has helped them find positive role models.*

explore their identity whilst also keeping themselves safe from those they don't want to know, or strangers on the internet. But all folks can choose to be private online to protect themselves, and some folks simply don't want to share their life with the online world.

Online hate speech and hate-crimes

Brook found that young LGBTQIA+ people described more benefits to digital technology but experienced more online risks. In the same survey, 73 per cent of LGBTQIA+ reported that they have been victims of online abuse, more than double the proportion among straight respondents.**

Many queer people experience hate speech online, whether that's directed at them as an individual, or at the wider community. If you've scrolled on Twitter/X for too long, you'll know that online anti-LGBTQIA+ hate speech is rampant. Hate speech can

---

* www.stonewall.org.uk/system/files/stonewall_staying_safe_online_april2022.pdf

** www.brook.org.uk/wp-content/uploads/2022/01/Digital-Intimacies-Summary-Report_BrookFINAL.pdf

happen publicly via social media posts or website forums, or privately through messaging and dating apps (we will come back to dating apps shortly!). Hate speech can be directed towards anyone, of any gender identity or sexuality, and it can also target multiple individuals and groups at once. However, Brook found that young LGBTQIA+ people also witness LGBTQIA+ adults pushing back against harassment, standing up for their fellow community members online.

As an openly trans person online, I face a heap of online abuse, comments, DMs, reposts, the lot. So much so that within the last year I asked someone I trusted to go through my comments and DMs and report or delete anything that may trigger me. He was a saint for doing so because I know how angry those comments made him, especially as they are directed towards me as an individual person. As I said, people feel that they can say anything they want because they are behind a screen and online hate is something many out LGBTQIA+ folks face. Many of these comments are made by trolls – people who post offensive, upsetting or inflammatory comments to hurt others. These comments may be considered a LGBTQIA+ hate crime, which is any crime that is targeted at a person because of prejudice based on the person's identity. Other examples of things which could be considered an online hate crime include:

⊙ Hate speech (as we just covered)
⊙ Trying to damage someone's reputation by making false comments
⊙ Accusing someone of doing things they didn't do
⊙ Stealing your identity
⊙ Setting up profiles in someone's name

- Doxing (publishing personal information about someone)
- Cyber-stalking
- Blackmail
- Encouraging further abuse or violence towards others.

WAIT, IT'S ILLEGAL TO OUT SOMEONE ONLINE?
LGBTQIA+ folks have the right to decide who knows about their sexual orientation and gender identity, as we have learnt. Outing someone without their consent is wrong and, in some cases, unlawful.

If someone outs you or discloses your gender history, sexual orientation or HIV status online, it may be unlawful if their actions are prohibited by a specific law or it is done to harass, blackmail or threaten you.*

Online dating

There are various ways people meet their partners. Through friends, at school or university, at work, through hobbies and, most commonly now, online.

First, back to the age of consent

Dating apps are age restricted, with most being for those aged 18 and over. There are a few out there that will allow younger folks to creep in (which isn't safe), but most will ban you if you're underage.

For many LGBTQIA+ people, online dating is sometimes the only form of dating available to them. Online dating means it's

---

* See www.tht.org.uk/get-help/living-well-hiv/support-people-living-hiv

BEYOND BANANAS AND CONDOMS

easier to find your dating pool, with most apps allowing you to cater your search to specific identities by giving you the option to share your own identity and identities you wish to match with. I loved online dating for a while as it meant people could see from my profile how I identified and what pronouns I used before swiping or starting a conversation; it ultimately got rid of those who didn't accept me without having to talk with them. And if you do match with someone who doesn't accept you, you can un-match or block them. Online dating also means you have an opportunity to think before you send. If you're an over-thinker like me, it can be beneficial to have some time before you press send.

DM slider

Now I'm not going to say I'm an expert, but I did hook, line and sinker a partner or two by sliding into their DMs. Here are Dee's DM slider tips:

- Be yourself – yes, you will find this tip in every 'how do I tell my crush I like them?' article or post, but if you do want something to come from this message then you want the person to like you for you. We know that social media isn't real, so let's not lie about ourselves to try to get someone to like or date us.
- If someone isn't into the DM or you, that's ok – not everyone you chat up will be into you and it's important you understand and accept that (remember consent and boundaries).
- Never share anything online you wouldn't want your gran to see – this is a rule for social media in general. It's important to not post or share something with someone, whether

that's a photo, a message or a fact that you wouldn't say in real life or wouldn't want someone close to you to see. This leads onto sexting but we will come onto that shortly.

◉ Sometimes liking someone's story is enough to catch their attention and start a conversation – it's perhaps the most common way my queer friends chat up people they fancy. If you are too shy to message someone directly, liking their story or photo could be enough of a trigger for them to message you!

Online dating can be just as romantic as meeting someone in-person; I think that the Covid lockdowns proved that it is completely possible to have healthy long-distance relationships with people. However, there are things we need to do to stay safe when it comes to online dating.

How do you turn down a DM slider?

Sometimes someone will slide into your DMs and you won't be vibing with them, and that's ok. If you don't want to chat with them, you can simply not reply, or if you do want to reply, let them know your boundaries. If they become aggressive because you turned them down, you can report them or block them.

Online dating for the gays

Brook also found in their Original Romance research that higher proportions of LGBTQIA+ young people have met a partner or asked someone out online.* Dating or having an online

---

* www.brook.org.uk/wp-content/uploads/2022/01/Digital-Intimacies-Summary-Report_BrookFINAL.pdf

relationship means you may only see or know a fraction about the individual you're chatting with, the fraction they want to share with you, which may not be 100 per cent true. And for LGBTQIA+ individuals, that may bring risks.

One of the best ways to enhance your safety when online dating as a queer person is to use an LGBTQIA+ dating app. Though this of course doesn't rule out all risk and dangers, it can limit them. It also provides a lower pressure environment where folks don't need to guess if someone they're into is queer.

If you're using a dating app, there are precautions you can take:

⊙ Check the app's terms of service – this will tell you about the app's privacy policy, and what happens with your data and information.

⊙ Check the safety precautions – some platforms have more trust and safety features than others, some apps include practices like identity verification, selfie verification and other sign-up features to make sure their users are real people (which can make it safer for LGBTQIA+ folks).

⊙ Check the app's reporting and policy features – this helps you to know that you can take your safety into your own hands if needed.

⊙ Read reviews of the app – bad reviews are a blessing!

'Let's talk about sexting, baby'

Sexting is the exchange of sexual messages or images, and the creating, sharing and forwarding of sexually suggestive nude or nearly nude images through mobile phones and the internet. I feel like we need a new term to replace 'sexting' because I only message on social media apps; who sends everyday photos via text anyway!?

To send a nude, or not to send a nude, that is the question... on some young people's minds. A 'nude' describes pictures of individuals which are taken completely nude or at some level undressed.

I want to be really clear, being nude is not inherently sexual, being nude is completely natural. Heck, we are born naked, and many folks feel empowered being in the nude in a non-sexual way. But when we talk about 'nudes', we typically mean images that are sexual in nature, sent for a sexual purpose, though that isn't always the case. Some trans folks take nudes of themselves to keep, whether to track their transition process, or to honour the body they previously had. But, mostly, people take nudes to send to someone. For example, folks that are dating may share nudes of themselves – also known as 'exchanging nudes' – as a way of flirting.

What does UK law say about sending nudes and sexting?

It's not illegal for adults to send nudes to other adults, as long as all parties consent to them. It is, however, illegal for someone over the age of 18 to have photos of anyone under the age of 18. It is also illegal for folks under the age of 18 to create or share sexual images of themselves or a peer (also under the age of 18). The fact the sender or person receiving the nude is under 18 does not affect the legal position – meaning it's illegal – though it's unlikely you will get into serious trouble, but it's certainly not worth the risk.

Here are some ways of initiating consensual sharing of nudes:

1. Ensure that both you and the other person want to send

and receive nudes; getting and giving consent is vital. Remember F – Freely given.

2. Check with them exactly what they feel comfortable and want to send/receive. As discussed in the consent chapter, the person must know everything about what they're engaging in before they can engage with it.

3. E – Enthusiasm – make sure the person is enthusiastic and wants to send/receive nudes; this means looking out for any hesitation, uncertainty or resistance. If they show any of this, or you feel any of this, then stop what you're doing.

4. If they say 'no' or anything along those lines, then accept their reply and move on with the conversation.

5. If you both want to send nudes, set ground rules. These can include how long the photos can stay in the chat for, whether they should be deleted or saved in a locked app afterwards, whether to include certain features such as faces etc.

Why might someone send nudes when they don't want to?

Sometimes people may feel pressured into sending a nude, intimidated, blackmailed or coerced – just as we spoke about in the consent chapter. Some folks may also feel obligated to do it because their partner is the one who asked them to send one, or because their partner sent them one first, so they feel almost as if they 'owe' them. Others may send a nude to 'fit in' with what their peers or friends are doing.

If this is the case, or if you regret sending a nude, don't panic (yes, easier said than done, but I had to say it). I want to remind you that you have done nothing wrong, though it may feel like it. We all make decisions we regret at some point in life. So, what should you do? First, it's important to speak with the person you sent the nude to. You should explain how you feel and ask them to delete it. The person should delete it from both the chat and their phone (being sure to delete it from their bin too). If the person refuses, there are steps you can take, like talking to a trusted adult or contacting the police. Talking to a trusted adult or parent about this may be an awkward conversation, even a scary one for some, but please remember that, if you're over the age of 18, sharing a nude is totally legal and anyone who shares that nude without your consent is in the wrong, not you. (Remember if you're under the age of 18, it is illegal for them to have that photo of you.) Even if the parent or trusted adult reacts in a bad way, it's important to remember that you're not the first to send a nude and you certainly won't be the last. Most of their reaction comes from a place of wanting to keep you safe, though it may not come across that way. If you're a parent or trusted adult and your young person or anyone has told you they have sent a nude, please refrain from being angry with them. Show your support, comfort them and actively try to help them. Shaming them or punishing them will only make them feel worse and mean they may not seek help from you in the future.

I've sent nudes. Most people I know have sent nudes or received them. Luckily none of mine were ever shared, though I will never know if they were fully deleted.

There is always a risk to sending nudes
There is no 100 per cent safe way to send a nude. Of course, the

laws around sexting and nudes are there to protect individuals, but this doesn't mean that sending nudes is completely risk-free. There are ways to take precautions when sending nudes, such as not including your face, or any recognizable tattoos or piercings or birthmarks, or your background/room in the photos. You should also only ever send nudes to someone you truly trust and know will listen to and respect your boundaries, storing the photos safely or deleting them afterwards. But it's important to remember that no matter how careful you are when sending nudes, there is always a risk the moment the photo or video is sent. We can't predict the future, so even if you send a nude to your long-term partner who you trust and love dearly, there is no guarantee that it will stay just between you both. Some social media sites also have ongoing access to whatever you share even after it's been deleted. People may also have their social media accounts hacked, meaning the hacker would have access to your messages and the photos you have sent (yes, it does happen!), so think before you send a photo or video on an app.

This is a message for my trans readers: please keep in mind that sending a nude of yourself pre-transition means that image may be out there for a long time or find its way into someone else's hands.

Cyber-flashing

Sometimes you may also receive a nude that you didn't want to receive... What do you do then? Unfortunately, many people I know, particularly girls, women and AFAB individuals, receive unwanted sexual images from people (mostly men and penis owners) of their genitals. A study carried out by Bumble in 2022 found that nearly half of women and AFAB folks ages 18 to 24 receive a sexual photo they didn't ask for.* I can't count on my hands how many unwanted penis shots I have received since being online, whether from a total stranger who thought 'they clearly want to see my penis at 2am' or from someone trying to flirt with me who thinks sending an unflattering shot of their penis next to a remote will turn me on. It is *never* ok to send a sexual image to someone without their consent, regardless of whether you know them, if they're your partner, or a total stranger, it's wrong. Not only is it wrong, it is also sexual harassment and called 'image-based sexual abuse'. And guess what? Cyber-flashing is now illegal in England and Wales. Through the Online Safety Bill, the government is also holding social media platforms accountable, placing more legal responsibility on them to keep their users safe from unwanted genital shots. These apps are supposed to do this, but often don't.

If you do receive an unwanted sexual image:

1. Take a screenshot of the message, so the username and photo are visible.
2. Store this screenshot safely, whether that's on a locked app or USB.
3. Tell the person who sent the unwanted photo that what they are doing is wrong and illegal.
4. Delete the chat, report the person and block them.
5. You can report this via Victim Support** or CEOP (Child Exploitation and Online Protection Command)*** if the person is underage.

---

* https://bumble.com/en/the-buzz/bumble-cyberflashing-law-uk-government-letter
** www.victimsupport.org.uk/crime-info/types-crime/sextortion
*** www.ceop.police.uk/Safety-Centre

Sometimes, you may receive a photo of someone you know. In this situation, take all the above steps but also reach out gently to the individual pictured to let them know what happened so that they can prepare themselves if others see the photo. Be sure to also tell them everything you've done to stop the sender from sending more photos and let them know that there is support out there.

> *But why would someone want to send your photo to other people or send you an unwanted photo of someone else?*
>
> People do this for a lot of different reasons: some folks want to show off to their friends, thinking it's cool; some may want to 'get back' at someone for breaking up with them or moving on, to cause shame and embarrassment, to laugh or mock the person. Some people may actively try to receive photos from people simply to share them on to harass them, pretending that they are interested romantically in the person to get what they want. Some people may take videos or photos of sexual assault and share or upload them. These people suck and what they are doing is illegal.

This is also called... revenge porn

Most people now use the term 'image-based sexual abuse' when talking about unwanted photos, but you may be more accustomed to hearing the term 'revenge porn'. However, the use of 'revenge' implies that the victim has done something to deserve it which is *never* the case, and the use of 'porn' implies that the victim was performing or wanted this photo to be circulated.

Korn... no, porn!

Porn is any form of material that is designed to cause sexual excitement, aka to turn someone on. This material includes images, videos, audio and writing (long-form and sexting). Porn often includes folks performing various sexual acts, in various states of nakedness, in various locations, with different numbers of folks, of varying identities, races and abilities, but some porn is also sensual, involving no sexual acts but rather sounds or role-play – there is porn out there for all kinds of folks regardless of how you identify. If you're into it, there will be porn of it.

So why do people watch porn? As I said, porn is mostly designed to turn someone on. People typically watch porn to masturbate to, or to get in the mood before having sex, watching it mutually with their partner/s. However, there is also a large proportion of people who use porn as an educational tool. Why? Because in-classroom sex education has let them down and porn seems like the best place to learn about sex... which isn't always the case. I want to start by saying that porn can be a great learning aid if you use ethical porn or porn that is designed to be consumed in an educational way, such as the material created by Beducated. Some people watch porn to see what certain body parts look like, body parts that they don't have, how certain sex positions look, or how LGBTQIA+ people have sex (you're not the first queer person to find out how gay folks have sex, and you won't be the last). However, most porn is not designed to be educational; it doesn't cover the topics we have explored in this book (consent, contraception etc) because it is purely for adult entertainment. Porn is not a 'how to guide', it isn't as in-depth as this book for example, and it can demonstrate dangerous practices to young people.

Porn isn't real (most of the time)

As I said, porn is adult entertainment, it is an act, a performance. An art form sometimes, but that means it isn't reality. Most of the time it's almost perfect looking, with ring-lights, perfect hair and makeup, in positions that most people simply can't bend into, moaning to the high heavens. There isn't any laughing, no smells, no messiness, or conversations about consent or contraception, or aftercare. Someone definitely doesn't run off to pee beforehand like I do every time or make jokes whilst putting on the condom – the conversations me and my sexual partners have had during sex would *never* make it into porn. Porn doesn't have some moments where erections go or someone can't climax – which is a very common occurrence right now for me as I'm taking antidepressants. We don't see conversations around dysphoria and what body parts are off-limits taking place. You don't see all the other parts that make sex, *sex*!

Porn can also push stereotypes, such as men and AMAB folks being dominant and hench, and women and AFAB folks being submissive and hairless in the bedroom. And of course, that may be some folks' truths, but if you see this specific way of having sex portrayed everywhere, you may think that that's the only way to have 'real sex'. It may force you into a position that you don't want to be in within the bedroom. Porn may also use terms that are discriminatory or derogatory for their genre headings, or within the actual porn video itself. Porn can also reinforce racist stereotypes. Black men and AMAB folks are presented as dominant, or aggressive, with large penises, whilst Asian individuals are portrayed as submissive and innocent. Folks are sexualized purely based on their race or ethnicity – this is called **racial fetishization**. Porn also doesn't represent all individuals' bodies, identities, backgrounds, faiths, needs etc – it can often be seen through just one lens – heterosexual, heteronormative and able-bodied. Most mainstream porn doesn't reflect disabled and neurodivergent individuals' experiences of sex.

Now we must talk about the darker side of porn, even darker than stereotypes and assumptions. There are some sites out there that show illegal content, content that is considered 'extreme pornography'. Porn that falls under this category includes: porn that puts anyone at risk, an act that causes serious and long-term harm to someone's body, sexual acts with a dead body or animal, porn showing anyone under the age of 18, and content of rape and sexual assault.

Now I'm not saying that porn is all bad; I love ethical porn.[*] As a trans queer person, porn has helped me to explore my gender identity and sexuality, it has helped me to feel more comfortable in my body seeing other trans folks have sex, and it's allowed me to share my tastes with my partners and vice versa. Porn can be great, but it's important to keep in mind the issues with the porn industry I have discussed and that porn is not real – it's a performance and real-life sex may not go as smoothly.

Am I a bad person if I watch porn?

As with all areas of sex, there will be things you enjoy and engage with, and things you don't. Porn is the same. Some folks enjoy

---

[*] What is ethical porn? Ethically produced porn is defined as porn made legally which respects the rights of the performers, has good working conditions, shows real-life sex and diversity. It isn't as performance-y as traditional porn, but it still isn't 100 per cent real-life as it's filmed. Ideally, all porn should be like this – but ethical porn requires more time and higher payments for performers, which is why most ethical porn is via smaller businesses or individual sex workers.

porn and that's totally ok, some folks don't like porn, and guess what, that's also ok. It doesn't make you a good or bad person, a better or worse person for watching or not watching porn. It just makes you a person! As we explored, as long as you're over the age of 18, consume ethical porn and understand that it isn't real, then you're a-ok! When I first started watching porn (on the family laptop, sorry mum and dad) I was terrified someone would find out, and most people feel the same way. But watching porn is completely natural and shouldn't be something we are ashamed of. That doesn't mean you need to watch it on your big TV in the living room for all to see, of course, privacy is still important, but it's certainly not something we should fear others knowing.

It's just as valid to not watch porn, or to find specific genres or tastes not for you. Not everyone is going to like the same porn you do, and there's a lot of different types of porn out there, so it would be impossible to engage with it all! You can explore different genres if you want to, because you may be into something you haven't tried yet, but don't feel as if you need to go through every category. Some folks simply don't want to engage with porn at all, for various reasons, and it's important to never feel pressured to watch porn because other people are. Only you get to decide whether you engage with porn.

Beyond
This Book

And that's all they wrote... for now

There is so much more I wish I could cover, but this book would be endless. It's also important to note that by the time this book is in your hands, there may be some sections which are outdated, new identities and acronyms added, new contraception, new pronouns – society is always changing, learning and unlearning, but I hope this book has provided you with a good foundation to jump off from. I'm excited to see what we have learnt in the time from writing this to publication! Please go out and read more sex ed books, continue your learning, because we (even us qualified sex educators) are learning new things every day – that's the beauty of sex ed and sexual health, it's forever developing! I hope I filled some gaps (or maybe all the gaps) that in-school sex education left you with, and I hope that by the time this book is on the shelves that young people have access to inclusive and comprehensive RSHE (Relationship and Sexual Health Education), which would mean books like mine are additional resources, not the only resource they have access to.

Refer to this book when you need to (because even I don't know all these facts off the top of my head); share this book with someone you know had a similar sex education to you, or a trans individual who received no sex ed that represented them. Our learning is a process, and it's one we can pass on, paying it forward to someone else who can then pay it forward to someone else. Or, if you don't want to share your copy, why not share a fun fact with them about the size of the clitoris, or teach them something new, like how small dick jokes are interphobic?

To my trans and gender-diverse+ folks

Your access to sex education is just as important as everyone else's. My mission for this book was to ensure you have the same amount of information and access to this resource as your cisgender peers. Though this book cannot be your sole source of sex education, and it shouldn't be. I hope by the time this book is on the shelves that it sits alongside other trans inclusive sex ed books. I want it to be part of a beautiful family of books all about your ins and outs because trans folks deserve more than just one sex ed book. At the time of writing this, the UK's sex education is under review, and we await a trans student guidance which will tell schools how to support their trans pupils; it is an uncertain time, but there are so many amazing LGBTQIA+ activists and sex ed advocates who are creating a safer and more accepting world within the sex ed sphere.

And if you think a specific community or existence is not being represented within the sex ed sphere, why not fill that gap?

My experience is that of a white, queer, trans, able-bodied, neurodivergent individual from London; my expertise within sex ed comes from a very specific background and this means I can't speak for all experiences – which is why a diverse round of voices within sex education activism is vital. If you don't see yourself in this space, put yourself in this space.

Sex education is our human right, and all individuals deserve to see themselves in their sex ed. And I hope you saw yourself in this book. Especially my trans youth.

By the way, I did finally have sex again! Go me.

Dee's Fave Resources

Sexual health/Sex ed

Brook
www.brook.org.uk
Brook operates a number of sexual health and wellbeing services across the UK.

Fumble
https://fumble.org.uk/about-us
Exciting, reliable digital content on intimacy, relationships, health and wellbeing. A happy, healthy digital world of free sex ed: created with young people, for young people.

School of Sexuality
https://schoolofsexed.org/useful-links
Support for schools to provide age-appropriate, inclusive, trauma-informed relationships and sex education programmes.

Revenge Porn Helpline
https://revengepornhelpline.org.uk
UK service supporting adults (aged 18+) who are experiencing intimate image abuse, also known as revenge porn.

Split Banana
https://splitbanana.co.uk/rse-workshops
Split Banana provides innovative relationship and sex education programmes to young people.

Sexual Health London
www.shl.uk
Sexual Health London is a discreet sexual health service for Londoners.

SH24
https://sh24.org.uk
Provides STI testing, diagnosis and treatment, oral contraception, the morning after pill and specialist remote clinical support.

SASH
www.sashlondon.org
SASH stands for Support and Advice on Sexual Health. Offers free, non-judgemental and confidential support to improve sexual health, relationships and mental health.

Gender

Mermaids
https://mermaidsuk.org.uk

The Trevor Project
www.thetrevorproject.org/resources/category/gender-identity

Terrence Higgins Trust
www.tht.org.uk/HIV-and-sexual-health/sexual-health/trans-people/resources

General LGBTQIA+ support

LGBT Foundation
https://lgbt.foundation
Delivers a wide range of services for lesbian, gay, bisexual and trans (LGBT) communities. They provide a variety of services, such as counselling, sexual health testing, social and support groups, drugs and alcohol support interventions, community safety initiatives, and befriending. In addition, they provide tailored programmes of support for lesbian and bisexual women, and for trans people, in light of the specific needs of these communities.

Gendered Intelligence
https://genderedintelligence.co.uk
Gendered Intelligence is a trans-led and trans-involving charity that works to increase understanding of gender diversity and improve the lives of trans people.

Stonewall
www.stonewall.org.uk
Stonewall is a lesbian, gay, bisexual and transgender rights charity in the UK.

The Proud Trust
www.theproudtrust.org
The Proud Trust is an LGBT+ organization that supports LGBT+ young people through youth groups, peer support, mentoring programmes and the Proud Connections.

AKT
www.akt.org.uk
Supporting homeless LGBTQIA+ folks.

Index

Note: page numbers followed by *f* indicate figures or diagrams

gay 90
and masturbation 162
'anti-trans' 20-1, 107-8
arguing 211
aromantic 91, 97, 175
arousal 41, 53
asexual 91-2
assigned sex 35, 117, 125
authority (power) 208
autoflexible 92

B

balls *see* testicles
'bananas and condoms' 13-14, 178f
barrier methods 177-84
Bartholin glands 42
behaviours
controlling 207-8
and gender 118-19
Benoit, Yasmin 91
bicurious 93
biflux 92
bigender 25
binding 85, 120-1
biological sex 35-6
Birkenstock sandals 116, 116f
biromantic 97
bisexual 18, 87, 93, 94
bleeding, irregular 49-50, 84
blood
during arousal 41, 53, 168-9
periods
abnormal 83-4
bleeding between 50, 187, 193
menstrual phase 77-8
'normal' amount 79, 85-6
rainbow of 83
and STIs 194, 195-6
blowjobs 158
'blue waffle' 198

body positivity 123-5
'born this way' slogan 106-7
bottom growth
cleaning 68
definition 54
as irreversible 68
minimizing 67
oral sex 157, 158
people likely to experience 67
surgery for 68
boundaries
around sex 149-50, 154
for online usage 217, 218-20
relationships 206, 212-13
setting 137, 212-13
break-ups
possible reasons for 213
tips for dumpees 215
tips for dumpers 214
Brook 134, 204, 221-2, 225, 240
bullying 98-9, 110
Butler, Judith 117
butt-plugs 164

C

cancers
in men, and people with penis
60-2
in women, and womb, cervix,
chest and vagina owners 46-52
casual sex 203-4
cervical cancer 47-9
cervical cap 183, 184
cervical screening 48-9
cervix 44f, 47-8, 81, 183, 184
cheating 210-11
cherry 43-4
chest
AMAB changes on oestrogen
HRT 69-70